P9-CAR-340

# KNOCK

## *Knock*

# WHO'S THERE?

*Good Clean Fun for Everyone*

Paul M. Miller

BARBOUR

PUBLISHING

© 2005 by Barbour Publishing, Inc.

ISBN 1-59310-691-2

All rights reserved. No part of this publication may be reproduced or transmitted for commercial purposes, except for brief quotations in printed reviews, without written permission of the publisher.

Churches and other noncommercial interests may reproduce portions of this book without the express written permission of Barbour Publishing, provided that the text does not exceed 500 words or 5 percent of the entire book, whichever is less, and that the text is not material quoted from another publisher. When reproducing text from this book, include the following credit line: "From *Knock-Knock—Who's There?* published by Barbour Publishing, Inc. Used by permission."

Cover image © Digital Vision

Published by Barbour Publishing, Inc., P.O. Box 719, Uhrichsville, Ohio 44683, www.barbourbooks.com

*Our mission is to publish and distribute inspirational products offering exceptional value and biblical encouragement to the masses.*

Member of the
Evangelical Christian
Publishers Association

Printed in the United States of America.
5 4 3 2

# CONTENTS

# INTRODUCTION

*Someone's at the Door!*
There isn't a parent, a teacher, a Sunday school superintendent, a kid, or a doting grandparent who hasn't experienced. . .

*Knock, knock*
*Who's there?*
*Boo!*
*Boo, who?*
*Well, you don't have to cry about it!*

Yep, the ever-living knock-knock joke.

Those who know say the pun is the lowest form of humor. If that's true, then the lowly knock-knock joke is relegated to the absolute pit of the lowest form of humor. But you know what? Nearly everyone agrees that a good knock-knock joke can knock the socks off an audience (even a strait-laced congregation) if the teller can stop laughing long enough to get the joke told.

Humor authority John F. Gilbey admits that knock-knock groaners have resisted the full press of a major fad because they are intellectually too demanding for most people. In other words, we who get a kick out of them are the real "intellectuals" of the world. (Read them aloud—it makes them easier to figure out.)

Can you believe this? Knock-knocks have so captured Charles Orr, a retiree living in Healdsburg, California, that he can boast of the largest collection of knock-knock jokes in the world. In the 1990s it was reported that he had catalogued 131,000 different knock-knocks, and was collecting and creating more every day.

What follows are a few hundred of the worst examples of the worst humor to be found anywhere. That's what will make this book a smash hit! These jokes are terrible—and you'll love 'em!

PAUL M. MILLER

# TAKIN' SOME KNOCKS

Knock, knock.
*Who's there?*
Atomic.
*Atomic who?*
I got atomic ache.

. . .

Knock, knock.
*Who's there?*
Weirdo.
*Weirdo who?*
Weirdo you think you're going?

Knock, knock.
*Who's there?*
Thermos.
*Thermos who?*
Thermos be a doorbell here some place.

· · ·

Knock, knock.
*Who's there?*
Ogre.
*Ogre who?*
Ogre there you'll find the gym.

· · ·

Knock, knock.
*Who's there?*
Unaware.
*Unaware who?*
Unaware is what you put on the first thing
 in the morning.

· · ·

Knock, knock.
*Who's there?*
Zany.
*Zany who?*
Zany body for Micky D's?

Knock, knock.
*Who's there?*
Astronaut.
*Astronaut who?*
Astronaut what your country can do for you,
  but what you can do for your country.

• • •

Knock, knock.
*Who's there?*
Lettuce.
*Lettuce who?*
Lettuce in—it's cold out here.

• • •

Knock, knock.
*Who's there?*
Izzy.
*Izzy who?*
Izzy come, Izzy go.

• • •

Knock, knock.
*Who's there?*
Cantaloupe.
*Cantaloupe who?*
But Charlie, we cantaloupe now!

Knock, knock.
*Who's there?*
Fanny.
*Fanny who?*
Fanny-body call, I don't want to talk.

• • •

Knock, knock.
*Who's there?*
Disguise.
*Disguise who?*
"Disguise falling!" warned Chicken Little.

• • •

Knock, knock.
*Who's there?*
Vaughn.
*Vaughn who?*
Vaughn, two, buckle my shoe!

• • •

Knock, knock.
*Who's there?*
Justin.
*Justin who?*
This Justin: Knock-knock jokes
to be forbidden by law.

Knock, knock.
*Who's there?*
Honey hive.
*Honey hive who?*
Honey, hive got a crush on you.

• • •

Knock, knock.
*Who's there?*
Andy.
*Andy who?*
Andy dish ran away with the spoon.

• • •

Knock, knock.
*Who's there?*
Juno.
*Juno who?*
Juno what time it is?

• • •

Knock, knock.
*Who's there?*
Wade.
*Wade who?*
Wade'll I make my first million!

Knock, knock.
*Who's there?*
Warrior.
*Warrior who?*
Warrior been? I've been knocking for hours!

• • •

Knock, knock.
*Who's there?*
Dishes.
*Dishes who?*
Dishes me. Who are you?

• • •

Knock, knock.
*Who's there?*
Henrietta and Juliet.
*Henrietta and Juliet who?*
Henrietta big dinner and got sick; Juliet the
    same, but she's fine.

• • •

Knock, knock.
*Who's there?*
Juicy.
*Juicy who?*
Juicy what I just saw?

Knock, knock.
*Who's there?*
Icy.
*Icy who?*
Icy no reason to keep me outside!

• • •

Knock, knock.
*Who's there?*
Dismay.
*Dismay who?*
Dismay seem funny, but I'm not laughing!

• • •

Knock, knock.
*Who's there?*
Thirst.
*Thirst who?*
Water is delivered on Thirst-day.

• • •

Knock, knock.
*Who's there?*
Donahue.
*Donahue who?*
Donahue hide from me, you coward.

Knock, knock.
*Who's there?*
Moose.
*Moose who?*
Urrrp. . .moose be something I ate.

• • •

Knock, knock.
*Who's there?*
Cereal.
*Cereal who?*
Cereal pleasure to meet you.

• • •

Knock, knock.
*Who's there?*
Lass.
*Lass who?*
Lass one to dinner is a rotten egg.

• • •

Knock, knock.
*Who's there?*
Howell.
*Howell who?*
Howell you have your hot dog—
with or without onions?

Knock, knock.
*Who's there?*
Papaya.
*Papaya who?*
Papaya the sailor man.

• • •

Knock, knock.
*Who's there?*
Dime.
*Dime who?*
Dime to tell another one of
these knock-knock jokes.

• • •

Knock, knock.
*Who's there?*
Gorilla.
*Gorilla who?*
Gorilla cheese sandwich.

• • •

Knock, knock.
*Who's there?*
Jonas.
*Jonas who?*
Jonas for a Coke after work.

Knock, knock.
*Who's there?*
Icon.
*Icon who?*
Icon tell you another one of these knock-
knock jokes.

. . .

Knock, knock.
*Who's there?*
Gruesome.
*Gruesome who?*
Gruesome tomatoes in my garden.

. . .

Knock, knock.
*Who's there?*
Unity.
*Unity who?*
Unity sweater for me?

. . .

Knock, knock.
*Who's there?*
Nobel.
*Nobel who?*
Nobel, so I knocked.

Knock, knock.
*Who's there?*
Vilma.
*Vilma who?*
Vilma frog turn into a prince?

. . .

Knock, knock.
*Who's there?*
Butter.
*Butter who?*
Butter let me in!

. . .

Knock, knock.
*Who's there?*
Tank.
*Tank who?*
You're welcome.

. . .

Knock, knock.
*Who's there?*
Safari.
*Safari who?*
Safari, so good.

Knock, knock.
*Who's there?*
Cotton.
*Cotton who?*
Cotton a trap—please help me.

. . .

Knock, knock.
*Who's there?*
Wendy Katz.
*Wendy Katz who?*
Wendy Katz away, the mice will play.

. . .

Knock, knock.
*Who's there?*
D-1.
*D-1 who?*
D-1 who knocked!

. . .

Knock, knock.
*Who's there?*
Ears.
*Ears who?*
Ears looking at you!

Knock, knock.
*Who's there?*
Ears.
*Ears who?*
Ears another knock-knock joke for you.

. . .

Knock, knock.
*Who's there?*
Pencil.
*Pencil who?*
Pencil fall down if I don't wear a belt.

. . .

Knock, knock.
*Who's there?*
Radio.
*Radio who?*
Radio not, here I come!

. . .

Knock, knock.
*Who's there?*
Zing.
*Zing who?*
Zing a song of sixpence, a pocket full of rye.

Knock, knock.
*Who's there?*
Scold.
*Scold who?*
Open the door—it scold out here!

• • •

Knock, knock.
*Who's there?*
B-2.
*B-2 who?*
Remember, B-2 school on time!

• • •

Knock, knock.
*Who's there?*
B-4.
*B-4 who?*
Open this door B-4 I freeze to death.

• • •

Knock, knock.
*Who's there?*
Repeat.
*Repeat who?*
Who. Who. Who!

Knock, knock.
*Who's there?*
Congo.
*Congo who?*
Congo out—I'm grounded.

•  •  •

Knock, knock.
*Who's there?*
Tori.
*Tori who?*
Tori seat of my pants. Help!

# HMM, YUM!

Knock, knock.
*Who's there?*
Ice cream soda.
*Ice cream soda who?*
Ice cream soda whole world will know what
a big nut you are.

. . .

Knock, knock.
*Who's there?*
Lemonade.
*Lemonade who?*
Lemonade me introduce you to my friend.

Knock, knock.
*Who's there?*
Almond.
*Almond who?*
Almond the side of the law.

• • •

Knock, knock.
*Who's there?*
Hominy.
*Hominy who?*
Hominy doughnuts can you eat?

• • •

Knock, knock.
*Who's there?*
Cashew.
*Cashew who?*
Cashew see I'm freezing out here?

• • •

Knock, knock.
*Who's there?*
Alec.
*Alec who?*
Alec my ice cream cone.

Knock, knock.
*Who's there?*
Candy.
*Candy who?*
Candy cow jump over the moon?

• • •

Knock, knock.
*Who's there?*
Grover.
*Grover who?*
Grover there and get me a cookie.

• • •

Knock, knock.
*Who's there?*
X.
*X who?*
Yum, X for breakfast!

• • •

Knock, knock.
*Who's there?*
Teresa.
*Teresa who?*
Teresa fly in my soup.

Knock, knock.
*Who's there?*
Cash.
*Cash who?*
I knew you were nuts.

• • •

Knock, knock.
*Who's there?*
Omelet.
*Omelet who?*
Omelet smarter than I look!

• • •

Knock, knock.
*Who's there?*
Frankfurter.
*Frankfurter who?*
Frankfurter lovely evening.

• • •

Knock, knock.
*Who's there?*
Turnip.
*Turnip who?*
Turnip the stereo—I can't hear it.

Knock, knock.
*Who's there?*
Irish Stew.
*Irish Stew who?*
Irish stew would stay for dinner.

. . .

Knock, knock.
*Who's there?*
Pizza.
*Pi    a who?*
Pizza that apple pie would be good.

. . .

Knock, knock.
*Who's there?*
Ice cream.
*Ice cream who?*
Ice cream every time I see a ghost.

. . .

Knock, knock.
*Who's there?*
Crummy.
*Crummy who?*
How the cookie felt when he went to the
doctor.

Knock, knock.
*Who's there?*
Butter.
*Butter who?*
I butter not tell you.

. . .

Knock, knock.
*Who's there?*
Closure.
*Closure who?*
Closure mouth when your eating!

. . .

Knock, knock.
*Who's there?*
Vitamin.
*Vitamin who?*
Vitamin for a party.

. . .

Knock, knock.
*Who's there?*
Orange.
*Orange who?*
Orange you going to open the door?

Knock, knock.
*Who's there?*
Doughnut.
*Doughnut who?*
Doughnut bother me with silly questions.

• • •

Knock, knock.
*Who's there?*
Banana.
*Banana who?*

Knock, knock.
*Who's there?*
Banana.
*Banana who?*

Knock, knock.
*Who's there?*
Orange.
*Orange who?*
Orange you glad I didn't say banana?

Knock, knock.
*Who's there?*
Pickle.
*Pickle who?*
Oh, that's my favorite musical instrument.

• • •

Knock, knock.
*Who's there?*
Irish stew.
*Irish stew who?*
Irish stew in the name of the law!

• • •

Knock, knock.
*Who's there?*
Cereal.
*Cereal who?*
Cereal soon.

• • •

Knock, knock.
*Who's there?*
Sandwiches.
*Sandwiches who?*
Sandwiches are scarier than sea witches.

Knock, knock.
*Who's there?*
Pear.
*Pear who?*
Pear-ables are teaching stories.

• • •

Knock, knock.
*Who's there?*
Pudding.
*Pudding who?*
Pudding on my overcoat—see you soon!

• • •

Knock, knock.
*Who's there?*
Alfredo sauce.
*Alfredo sauce who?*
Alfredo sauce-um flying saucers.

• • •

Knock, knock.
*Who's there?*
Ginger punch.
*Ginger punch who?*
Ginger punch-ed 'em out!

# A-LIST GIRLS

Knock, knock.
*Who's there?*
Alicia.
*Alicia who?*
Alicia like me a little bit, don't you?

. . .

Knock, knock.
*Who's there?*
Ada.
*Ada who?*
Ada burger for lunch.

Knock, knock.
*Who's there?*
Abby.
*Abby who?*
Abby birthday to you!

. . .

Knock, knock.
*Who's there?*
Alfreda.
*Alfreda who?*
Alfreda the dark.

. . .

Knock, knock.
*Who's there?*
Anna.
*Anna who?*
Anna 'nother mosquito.

. . .

Knock, knock.
*Who's there?*
Alison.
*Alison who?*
Alison to the radio in my car.

Knock, knock.
*Who's there?*
Anna.
*Anna who?*
Anna one, Anna two. . .

• • •

Knock, knock.
*Who's there?*
Annie.
*Annie who?*
Annie one you like.

• • •

Knock, knock.
*Who's there?*
Anita.
*Anita who?*
Anita borrow a pencil.

• • •

Knock, knock.
*Who's there?*
Agatha.
*Agatha who?*
Agatha feeling you're foolin'.

Knock, knock.
*Who's there?*
Abby.
*Abby who?*
Abby good if you'll give me a flower.

• • •

Knock, knock.
*Who's there?*
Amanda.
*Amanda who?*
Amanda wants to give you a big kiss.

• • •

Knock, knock.
*Who's there?*
Anita.
*Anita who?*
Anita great big hug.

• • •

Knock, knock.
*Who's there?*
Annie.
*Annie who?*
Annie reason you're not letting me in?

Knock, knock.
*Who's there?*
Anita.
*Anita who?*
Anita a tissue. *Ah choo!*

• • •

Knock, knock.
*Who's there?*
Ashley.
*Ashley who?*
Ashley, it's none of your business.

• • •

Knock, knock.
*Who's there?*
Athena.
*Athena who?*
Athena flying saucer.

• • •

Knock, knock.
*Who's there?*
Augusta.
*Augusta who?*
Augusta wind blew my hat off.

Knock, knock.
*Who's there?*
Albie.
*Albie who?*
Albie back—don't you forget.

• • •

Knock, knock.
*Who's there?*
Arlis.
*Arlis who?*
Arlis of overdue books is long.

• • •

Knock, knock.
*Who's there?*
Audra.
*Audra who?*
Audra whatever you want to draw.

• • •

Knock, knock.
*Who's there?*
Aileen.
*Aileen who?*
Aileen piece of meat is good for
the waistline.

Knock, knock.
*Who's there?*
Agnes C.
*Agnes C. who?*
The Agnes C. and the Ecstasy.

• • •

Knock, knock.
*Who's there?*
Angela.
*Angela who?*
Los Angeles is a huge city.

• • •

Knock, knock.
*Who's there?*
Arlene.
*Arlene who?*
Arlene boys stronger than fat ones?

• • •

Knock, knock.
*Who's there?*
Alexa.
*Alexa who?*
Alexa to open the door just one more time.

Knock, knock.
*Who's there?*
Anna.
*Anna who?*
"Anna He walks with me, Anna He talks
with me. . ."

. . .

Knock, knock.
*Who's there?*
Alberta.
*Alberta who?*
Alberta and Joe Berta are cousins.

. . .

Knock, knock.
*Who's there?*
Aletha.
*Aletha who?*
Aletha good breakfast, and feel good all day.

. . .

Knock, knock.
*Who's there?*
Alma.
*Alma who?*
Alma woman of mystery.

Knock, knock.
*Who's there?*
Ada.
*Ada who?*
Ada person in distress.

. . .

Knock, knock.
*Who's there?*
Alice.
*Alice who?*
Alice stay for a cup of cocoa, please?

. . .

Knock, knock.
*Who's there?*
Anita.
*Anita who?*
Anita you to let me in.

# CELEBS

Knock, knock.
*Who's there?*
Anwar.
*Anwar who?*
Anwar sorry about the rain delay.

* * *

Knock, knock.
*Who's there?*
Eisenhower.
*Eisenhower who?*
Eisenhower late for school.

Knock, knock.
*Who's there?*
Abraham Lincoln.
*Abraham Lincoln who?*
Come on now, there's only one Abraham
    Lincoln.

. . .

Knock, knock.
*Who's there?*
Gravy.
*Gravy who?*
Gravy Crockett.

. . .

Knock, knock.
*Who's there?*
Soup.
*Soup who?*
Souperman.

. . .

Knock, knock.
*Who's there?*
Atom.
*Atom who?*
Atom and Eve.

Knock, knock.
*Who's there?*
Custer.
*Custer who?*
Custer or cream cheese?

. . .

Knock, knock.
*Who's there?*
Hussein.
*Hussein who?*
Hussein in the mental hospital?

. . .

Knock, knock.
*Who's there?*
Clark Kent.
*Clark Kent who?*
Clark Kent come—he's sick.

. . .

Knock, knock.
*Who's there?*
Alex.
*Alex who?*
Alex in Wonderland.

Knock, knock.
*Who's there?*
Whittle.
*Whittle who?*
Whittle Orphan Annie.

• • •

Knock, knock.
*Who's there?*
Bach.
*Bach who?*
Bach in five minutes.

• • •

Knock, knock.
*Who's there?*
Wilbur Wright.
*Wilbur Wright who?*
Wilbur Wright back after these commercials.

• • •

Knock, knock.
*Who's there?*
Caesar.
*Caesar who?*
Caesar a jolly good fellow.

Knock, knock.
*Who's there?*
Atlas.
*Atlas who?*
Atlas it's the weekend!

. . .

Knock, knock.
*Who's there?*
Atlas.
*Atlas who?*
Atlas we're alone.

. . .

Knock, knock.
*Who's there?*
Gable.
*Gable who?*
Gable to leap buildings in a single bound.

. . .

Knock, knock.
*Who's there?*
Marcus Welby.
*Marcus Welby who?*
Marcus Welby dead for all you care.

Knock, knock.
*Who's there?*
Nadia.
*Nadia who?*
Nadia believe me?

• • •

Knock, knock.
*Who's there?*
King Kong.
*King Kong who?*
King Kong the witch is dead.

• • •

Knock, knock.
*Who's there?*
Ben Hur.
*Ben Hur who?*
Ben Hur an hour an' she ain't in sight.

• • •

Knock, knock.
*Who's there?*
Descartes.
*Descartes who?*
Don't put Descartes before de horse.

Knock, knock.
*Who's there?*
Gunga Din.
*Gunga Din who?*
Gunga Din free, 'cuz I know the usher.

· · ·

Knock, knock.
*Who's there?*
Punch!
*Punch who?*
Not me! I just got here!

· · ·

Knock, knock.
*Who's there?*
Mahatma.
*Mahatma who?*
Mahatma coat, please.

· · ·

Knock, knock.
*Who's there?*
E. T.
*E. T. who?*
E. T. your food before it gets cold.

Knock, knock.
*Who's there?*
Tom Sawyer.
*Tom Sawyer who?*
Tom Sawyer holey sock.

• • •

Knock, knock.
*Who's there?*
Romeo.
*Romeo who?*
Romeo cross the lake in your boat.

• • •

Knock, knock.
*Who's there?*
Sloan.
*Sloan who?*
Sloan Ranger rides again!

• • •

Knock, knock.
*Who's there?*
Yoda.
*Yoda who?*
Yoda best!

Knock, knock.
*Who's there?*
Desdemona.
*Desdemona who?*
Desdemona Lisa still hang in Paris?

. . .

Knock, knock.
*Who's there?*
Aladdin.
*Aladdin who?*
Aladdin the street wants a word with you.

. . .

Knock, knock.
*Who's there?*
Olive.
*Olive who?*
Olive Spiderman.

. . .

Knock, knock.
*Who's there?*
Barbie.
*Barbie who?*
Will you come to my Barbie Q?

Knock, knock.
*Who's there?*
Aretha.
*Aretha who?*
I have Aretha flowers in my hair.

. . .

Knock, knock.
*Who's there?*
Anne Boleyn.
*Anne Boleyn who?*
Anne Boleyn alley.

. . .

Knock, knock.
*Who's there?*
Ptolemy.
*Ptolemy who?*
Ptolemy that you love me.

. . .

Knock, knock.
*Who's there?*
Avis.
*Avis who?*
Avis-itor from Mars!

Knock, knock.
*Who's there?*
Deduct.
*Deduct who?*
Donald deduct.

. . .

Knock, knock.
*Who's there?*
Albee.
*Albee who?*
Well, Albee a monkey's uncle.

. . .

Knock, knock.
*Who's there?*
Jack.
*Jack who?*
Jack be nimble, Jack be quick.

. . .

Knock, knock.
*Who's there?*
Aida.
*Aida who?*
Aida lot of sweets—
now I have a tummy ache.

Knock, knock.
*Who's there?*
It's Tom Thumb.
*It's Tom Thumb who?*
It's Tom Thumb-ody open this door!

•  •  •

Knock, knock.
*Who's there?*
Art.
*Art who?*
Art 2-D-2.

•  •  •

Knock, knock.
*Who's there?*
Apollo.
*Apollo who?*
Sorry—I apollo-gize!

•  •  •

Knock, knock.
*Who's there?*
Euripides.
*Euripides who?*
Euripides pants, and you'll buy him a new
pair!

Knock, knock.
*Who's there?*
Twain.
*Twain who?*
A Twain is what wabbits take a twip on.

. . .

Knock, knock.
*Who's there?*
Zeus.
*Zeus who?*
Zeus house is this anyway?

. . .

Knock, knock.
*Who's there?*
Houdini.
*Houdini who?*
Houdini invite to church?

. . .

Knock, knock.
*Who's there?*
Midas.
*Midas who?*
Midas well sit down.

Knock, knock.
*Who's there?*
Oblong.
*Oblong who?*
Oblong Cassidy. Were you expecting Roy
    Rogers?

. . .

Knock, knock.
*Who's there?*
Aesop.
*Aesop who?*
Aesop I saw a puddy tat.

. . .

Knock, knock.
*Who's there?*
Don Giovanni.
*Don Giovanni who?*
Don Giovanni come out and play?

. . .

Knock, knock.
*Who's there?*
Sonny and Cher.
*Sonny and Cher who?*
Sonny and Cher to be cloudy later.

Knock, knock.
*Who's there?*
Don Juan.
*Don Juan who?*
Don Juan to keep knocking—open the door!

• • •

Knock, knock.
*Who's there?*
Oscar.
*Oscar who?*
Oscar for a date,
and maybe she'll go out with you.

• • •

Knock, knock.
*Who's there?*
I'm Cher.
*I'm Cher who?*
I'm Cher I don't wanna be standing out
here—open up!

# NAME GAME

Knock, knock.
*Who's there?*
Theodore.
*Theodore who?*
Theodore got slammed on my nose.

• • •

Knock, knock.
*Who's there?*
Morgan.
*Morgan who?*
Afraid I'm Morgan you can put up with.

Knock, knock.
*Who's there?*
Orson.
*Orson who?*
Orson wagon are parked outside.

• • •

Knock, knock.
*Who's there?*
Mickey.
*Mickey who?*
Mickey is stuck in the lock. I need help!

• • •

Knock, knock.
*Who's there?*
Keith.
*Keith who?*
Keith your dog on a leash.

• • •

Knock, knock.
*Who's there?*
Ivan.
*Ivan who?*
Ivan my money back!

Knock, knock.
*Who's there?*
Randy.
*Randy who?*
Randy four minute mile in less than three.

• • •

Knock, knock.
*Who's there?*
Alfie.
*Alfie who?*
Alfie you later.

• • •

Knock, knock.
*Who's there?*
Norm.
*Norm who?*
Norm-ally these jokes are funnier.

• • •

Knock, knock.
*Who's there?*
Otto.
*Otto who?*
Otto thieving is a serious crime.

Knock, knock.
*Who's there?*
Stan.
*Stan who?*
Stan back, I'm kicking the door down!

．．．

Knock, knock.
*Who's there?*
Alistair.
*Alistair who?*
Alistair at the TV and fall asleep.

．．．

Knock, knock.
*Who's there?*
Dewey.
*Dewey who?*
Dewey have to keep telling these dumb
jokes?

．．．

Knock, knock.
*Who's there?*
Emil.
*Emil who?*
Emil fit for a king.

Knock, knock.
*Who's there?*
Oly.
*Oly who?*
"Oly to bed, Oly to rise. . ."

. . .

Knock, knock.
*Who's there?*
Seymour.
*Seymour who?*
Seymour of your friends
if you'd open the door.

. . .

Knock, knock.
*Who's there?*
Xavier.
*Xavier who?*
Xavier breath, I said no!

. . .

Knock, knock.
*Who's there?*
Arthur.
*Arthur who?*
Arthur any more at home like you?

Knock, knock.
*Who's there?*
Earl.
*Earl who?*
Earl be glad to tell when you open the door.

. . .

Knock, knock.
*Who's there?*
Panther.
*Panther who?*
Panther no panth, I'm going swimming.

. . .

Knock, knock.
*Who's there?*
Hutch.
*Hutch who?*
God bless you!

. . .

Knock, knock.
*Who's there?*
Alfie.
*Alfie who?*
Alfie terrible if you leave.

Knock, knock.
*Who's there?*
Sorry, sorry! I've forgotten the rest of the
  joke.
*Sorry, sorry! I've forgotten the rest of the joke
who?*
No! I've forgotten the dumb joke!

• • •

Knock, knock.
*Who's there?*
Abbott.
*Abbott who?*
Abbott time you answered the door.

• • •

Knock, knock.
*Who's there?*
Arch.
*Arch who?*
You catching a cold?

• • •

Knock, knock.
*Who's there?*
Toby.
*Toby who?*
"Toby, or not to be. . ."

Knock, knock.
*Who's there?*
Dwayne.
*Dwayne who?*
Dwayne the bath tub, I'm drowning!

• • •

Knock, knock.
*Who's there?*
Amory.
*Amory who?*
Amory Christmas and a Happy New Year.

• • •

Knock, knock.
*Who's there?*
Alvin.
*Alvin who?*
Alvin a great time, how about you?

• • •

Knock, knock.
*Who's there?*
Al.
*Al who?*
Al give you a kiss if you open this door.

Knock, knock.
*Who's there?*
Tobias.
*Tobias who?*
Tobias some rocky road ice cream.

• • •

Knock, knock.
*Who's there?*
Arnold.
*Arnold who?*
Arnold friend you haven't seen for years.

• • •

Knock, knock.
*Who's there?*
Max.
*Max who?*
Max no difference.

• • •

Knock, knock.
*Who's there?*
Dewey.
*Dewey who?*
Dewey have to go to the dentist?

Knock, knock.
*Who's there?*
Stan.
*Stan who?*
Stan up straight and stop slouching!

• • •

Knock, knock.
*Who's there?*
Arnie.
*Arnie who?*
Arnie having fun yet?

• • •

Knock, knock.
*Who's there?*
Thayer.
*Thayer who?*
Thayer sorry, and I won't tell teacher.

• • •

Knock, knock.
*Who's there?*
Otto.
*Otto who?*
You Otto know, I can't remember.

Knock, knock.
*Who's there?*
Archibald.
*Archibald who?*
Archibald on the top of your head?

. . .

Knock, knock.
*Who's there?*
Arthur.
*Arthur who?*
Arthur any more cookies in the jar?

. . .

Knock, knock.
*Who's there?*
Irving.
*Irving who?*
Irving a good time. Wish you were here!

. . .

Knock, knock.
*Who's there?*
Wayne.
*Wayne who?*
Wayne are we gonna eat? I'm starving!

Knock, knock.
*Who's there?*
Watson.
*Watson who?*
Nothing much. Watson who with you?

. . .

Knock, knock.
*Who's there?*
Alec.
*Alec who?*
Alec-tricity. Isn't that a shock?

. . .

Knock, knock.
*Who's there?*
Warner.
*Warner who?*
Warner go to a movie with me?

. . .

Knock, knock.
*Who's there?*
Eddie.
*Eddie who?*
Eddie body home?

Knock, knock.
*Who's there?*
Watson.
*Watson who?*
What's on the table? I'm hungry.

. . .

Knock, knock.
*Who's there?*
Bruce.
*Bruce who?*
I Bruce some tea for us.

# OLDIES
# BUT
# GOODIES

Knock, knock.
*Who's there?*
Ina Claire.
*Ina Claire who?*
"Ina Claire day you can see forever."

• • •

Knock, knock.
*Who's there?*
India.
*India who?*
"India good ol' summer time."

Knock, knock.
*Who's there?*
Dwayne.
*Dwayne who?*
"Dwayne in Spain falls mainly on the plain."

. . .

Knock, knock.
*Who's there?*
Agatha.
*Agatha who?*
"Agatha blues in the night."

. . .

Knock, knock.
*Who's there?*
Luke.
*Luke who?*
"Luke for the silver lining."

. . .

Knock, knock.
*Who's there?*
Peephole.
*Peephole who?*
"Peephole who need people."

Knock, knock.
*Who's there?*
A Fred!
*A Fred who?*
"Who's a Fred of the big bad wolf?"

. . .

Knock, knock.
*Who's there?*
Don Ameche.
*Don Ameche who?*
"I'll be Don Ameche in a taxi honey."

. . .

Knock, knock.
*Who's there?*
Don Juan.
*Don Juan who?*
"I Don Juan to set the world on fire."

. . .

Knock, knock.
*Who's there?*
Donna.
*Donna who?*
"Donna sit under the apple tree."

Knock, knock.
*Who's there?*
Wayne.
*Wayne who?*
"Wayne dwops keep falling on my head."

• • •

Knock, knock.
*Who's there?*
Freeze.
*Freeze who?*
"Freeze a jolly good fellow."

• • •

Knock, knock.
*Who's there?*
Alice.
*Alice who?*
"I'm Alice chasing rainbows."

• • •

Knock, knock.
*Who's there?*
Gnome.
*Gnome who?*
"Gnome-body knows the trouble I've seen."

Knock, knock.
*Who's there?*
Greta.
*Greta who?*
"Greta long little doggie, get along."

· · ·

Knock, knock.
*Who's there?*
Heifer.
*Heifer who?*
"If heifer I should leave you."

· · ·

Knock, knock.
*Who's there?*
Hummus.
*Hummus who?*
"Hummus remember this, a kiss is just a kiss."

· · ·

Knock, knock.
*Who's there?*
Hyman.
*Hyman who?*
"Hyman the mood for love."

Knock, knock.
*Who's there?*
Jose.
*Jose who?*
"Jose can you see, by the dawn's early light?"

•  •  •

Knock, knock.
*Who's there?*
Oil can.
*Oil can who?*
"My oil can-tucky home."

•  •  •

Knock, knock.
*Who's there?*
Sam and Janet.
*Sam and Janet who?*
"Sam and Janet evening."

•  •  •

Knock, knock.
*Who's there?*
Shelby.
*Shelby who?*
"Shelby coming around the mountain
when she comes."

Knock, knock.
*Who's there?*
Picasso.
*Picasso who?*
"Picasso you, there's a song in my heart."

• • •

Knock, knock.
*Who's there?*
Kelly.
*Kelly who?*
"Kelly-fornia here I come."

• • •

Knock, knock.
*Who's there?*
Mary Lee.
*Mary Lee who?*
"Mary Lee we roll along."

• • •

Knock, knock.
*Who's there?*
Venue.
*Venue who?*
"Venue vish upon a star."

Knock, knock.
*Who's there?*
Police.
*Police who?*
"Police don't talk about me when I'm gone."

• • •

Knock, knock.
*Who's there?*
Owl.
*Owl who?*
"Owl be seeing you,
in all the old familiar places."

• • •

Knock, knock.
*Who's there?*
One shoe.
*One shoe who?*
"One shoe come home Bill Bailey."

• • •

Knock, knock.
*Who's there?*
S-Two.
*S-Two who?*
"S-Two be a morning after."

Knock, knock.
*Who's there?*
Grace.
*Grace who?*
"Grace skies are gonna clear up, put on a
    happy face."

. . .

Knock, knock.
*Who's there?*
Crow.
*Crow who?*
"Crow, crow, crow your boat."

. . .

Knock, knock.
*Who's there?*
Ammonia.
*Ammonia who?*
"Ammonia bird in a gilded cage."

. . .

Knock, knock.
*Who's there?*
Igloo.
*Igloo who?*
"Igloo knew Suzie like I know Suzie."

Knock, knock.
*Who's there?*
Ketchup.
*Ketchup who?*
"Ketchup falling star and put it in your
    pocket."

. . .

Knock, knock.
*Who's there?*
Ike.
*Ike who?*
"Ike could have danced all night."

. . .

Knock, knock.
*Who's there?*
Akron.
*Akron who?*
"Akron give you anything but love, baby."

. . .

Knock, knock.
*Who's there?*
Agatha.
*Agatha who?*
"Agatha the world on a string."

Knock, knock.
*Who's there?*
Fido.
*Fido who?*
"Fido known you were coming I'da baked a
  cake."

. . .

Knock, knock.
*Who's there?*
Amahl.
*Amahl who?*
"Amahl shook up."

. . .

Knock, knock.
*Who's there?*
Saddle.
*Saddle who?*
"Saddle be the day when I die."

. . .

Knock, knock.
*Who's there?*
Laurie.
*Lauri who?*
"Laurie, Laurie hallelujah."

Knock, knock.
*Who's there?*
Shannon.
*Shannon who?*
"Shannon, Shannon harvest moon, up in the
   sky."

• • •

Knock, knock.
*Who's there?*
Menu.
*Menu who?*
"Menu wish upon a star."

# PEW PUNS

Knock, knock.
*Who's there?*
Andy.
*Andy who?*
"Andy walks with me, and He talks with
    me. . ."

. . .

Knock, knock.
*Who's there?*
Decanter.
*Decanter who?*
Decanter at my synagogue must be
80 years old.

Knock, knock.
*Who's there?*
Uriah and Uriah.
*Uriah and Uriah who?*
Uriahs are beautiful.

. . .

Knock, knock.
*Who's there?*
Manny.
*Manny who?*
"Manny are called, but few are chosen."

. . .

Knock, knock.
*Who's there?*
Isaiah.
*Isaiah who?*
Isaiah nothing without my lawyer!

. . .

Knock, knock.
*Who's there?*
Ezra.
*Ezra who?*
Ezra anybody home?

Knock, knock.
*Who's there?*
Luke.
*Luke who?*
"Luke and live, my brother live."

. . .

Knock, knock.
*Who's there?*
Goliath.
*Goliath who?*
Goliath down. Thou lookest tired.

. . .

Knock, knock.
*Who's there?*
Osmosis.
*Osmosis who?*
Osmosis, that's who I am.

. . .

Knock, knock.
*Who's there?*
I love.
*I love who?*
I don't know, but I love Jesus.

Knock, knock.
*Who's there?*
Lettuce.
*Lettuce who?*
Lettuce pray.

. . .

Knock, knock.
*Who's there?*
Zeke.
*Zeke who?*
"Zeke and ye shall find."

. . .

Knock, knock.
*Who's there?*
Gandhi.
*Gandhi who?*
"Gandhi walks with me, and He talks with
    me."

. . .

Knock, knock.
*Who's there?*
Bess.
*Bess who?*
"Bess be the tie that binds."

Knock, knock.
*Who's there?*
Nun.
*Nun who?*
Nun of these things will hurt you.

• • •

Knock, knock.
*Who's there?*
Ark.
*Ark who?*
Ark-tic ice is for penguins.

• • •

Knock, knock.
*Who's there?*
Zenda.
*Zenda who?*
"Zenda walls came tumbling down."

• • •

Knock, knock.
*Who's there?*
Armageddon.
*Armageddon who?*
Armageddon out of here!

Knock, knock.
*Who's there?*
Deuteronomy.
*Deuteronomy who?*
Deuteronomy problems, I'm staying home
from youth group.

• • •

Knock, knock.
*Who's there?*
John 1.
*John 1 who?*
John 1 the Sunday school contest.

• • •

Knock, knock.
*Who's there?*
Heaven.
*Heaven who?*
Heaven seen you for ages.

• • •

Knock, knock.
*Who's there?*
I, Felix.
*I, Felix who?*
I, Felix-cited.

Knock, knock.
*Who's there?*
Shallow.
*Shallow who?*
"Shallow we gather at the river?"

. . .

Knock, knock.
*Who's there?*
Esau.
*Esau who?*
Esau you come in last night.

. . .

Knock, knock.
*Who's there?*
Amen.
*Amen who?*
Amen and the women sang in the choir.

. . .

Knock, knock.
*Who's there?*
Saul.
*Saul who?*
Saul the king's men.

Knock, knock.
*Who's there?*
Urn.
*Urn who?*
"Urn your eyes upon Jesus."

. . .

Knock, knock.
*Who's there?*
Matthew.
*Matthew who?*
Matthew love, English I hate.

. . .

Knock, knock.
*Who's there?*
Daniel.
*Daniel who?*
Daniel have to take care of those lions.

. . .

Knock, knock.
*Who's there?*
Amen.
*Amen who?*
Amen deep trouble again!

Knock, knock.
*Who's there?*
Amos.
*Amos who?*
Amos-quito bit me.

. . .

Knock, knock.
*Who's there?*
Seth.
*Seth who?*
Seth me, and what I say goes.

. . .

Knock, knock.
*Who's there?*
Andy.
*Andy who?*
Andy will make us fishers of men.

. . .

Knock, knock.
*Who's there?*
Shirley.
*Shirley who?*
"Shirley goodness and mercy shall follow me
all the days of my life."

Knock, knock.
_Who's there?_
Andrew.
_Andrew who?_
Andrew all over the wall!

• • •

Knock, knock.
_Who's there?_
Noah.
_Noah who?_
Noah good place to eat?

• • •

Knock, knock.
_Who's there?_
The cross-eyed bear.
_The cross-eyed bear who?_
"Gladly the cross-eyed bear."

• • •

Knock, knock.
_Who's there?_
Pharaoh.
_Pharaoh who?_
Pharaoh foul, this is baseball.

Knock, knock.
*Who's there?*
Shaddrack.
*Shaddrack who?*
A Shaddrack is about the same as a fish
    rack.

• • •

Knock, knock.
*Who's there?*
Psalm.
*Psalm who?*
Psalm of you ought to go to church.

• • •

Knock, knock.
*Who's there?*
Hymn.
*Hymn who?*
Hymn and her ought to go together.

• • •

Knock, knock.
*Who's there?*
Noah.
*Noah who?*
"Noah-body knows the trouble I've seen."

Knock, knock.
*Who's there?*
Ark.
*Ark who?*
"Ark the Harold angels sing!"

•  •  •

Knock, knock.
*Who's there?*
Ox.
*Ox who?*
"Ox for me and my house,
we will serve the Lord."

•  •  •

Knock, knock.
*Who's there?*
Pastor.
*Pastor who?*
"He makes me lie down in green pastors."

•  •  •

Knock, knock.
*Who's there?*
Abner.
*Abner who?*
Abner-cadabra!

Knock, knock.
*Who's there?*
Uriah.
*Uriah who?*
Keep Uriah on the ball.

•   •   •

Knock, knock.
*Who's there?*
Heavenly.
*Heavenly who?*
Heavenly met somewhere before?

•   •   •

Knock, knock.
*Who's there?*
Phillip.
*Phillip who?*
Phillip the tank, please.

•   •   •

Knock, knock.
*Who's there?*
Evan.
*Evan who?*
"Evan and earth shall pass away, but My
Word will not."

Knock, knock.
*Who's there?*
Pastor.
*Pastor who?*
She pastor finals in math?

. . .

Knock, knock.
*Who's there?*
Gideon.
*Gideon who?*
Gideon your horse and let's go!

. . .

Knock, knock.
*Who's there?*
Aaron.
*Aaron who?*
Aaron out my stinky gym bag.

# 'TIS
# THE
# SEASON

Knock, knock.
*Who's there?*
Snow.
*Snow who?*
Snow skating today, the ice is thin.

. . .

Knock, knock.
*Who's there?*
Wayne.
*Wayne who?*
"Wayne in a manger, no crib for a bed."

Knock, knock.
*Who's there?*
Doughnut.
*Doughnut who?*
Doughnut open until Christmas.

. . .

Knock, knock.
*Who's there?*
Autumn.
*Autumn who?*
Autumn-y ache is almost gone.

. . .

Knock, knock.
*Who's there?*
Summertime.
*Summertime who?*
Summertime you win, summertime you lose.

. . .

Knock, knock.
*Who's there?*
Rain.
*Rain who?*
Rain, rain, go away, come again
some other day.

Knock, knock.
*Who's there?*
Turkey.
*Turkey who?*
Turkey was lost, but she found it.

• • •

Knock, knock.
*Who's there?*
Santa Ana.
*Santa Ana who?*
Santa Ana gonna bring you anything if
you're naughty.

• • •

Knock, knock.
*Who's there?*
Firecrackers.
*Firecrackers who?*
Firecrackers, but water makes it quiet.

• • •

Knock, knock.
*Who's there?*
Fresno.
*Fresno who?*
Rudolf the Fresno-sed reindeer.

Knock, knock.
*Who's there?*
Holly.
*Holly who?*
"O, holly night, the stars were brightly
    shining."

• • •

Knock, knock.
*Who's there?*
Hurricanes.
*Hurricanes who?*
Hurricanes to the old folks home.

• • •

Knock, knock.
*Who's there?*
Calendar.
*Calendar who?*
Calendar you to make some resolutions.

• • •

Knock, knock.
*Who's there?*
Trigger.
*Trigger who?*
Trigger treat!

Knock, knock.
*Who's there?*
Fortification.
*Fortification who?*
Fortification I go to the seashore every
    summer.

· · ·

Knock, knock.
*Who's there?*
Hannah.
*Hannah who?*
"Hannah partridge in a pear tree."

· · ·

Knock, knock.
*Who's there?*
One.
*One who?*
One-derful day, isn't it?

· · ·

Knock, knock.
*Who's there?*
Felix.
*Felix who?*
Felix-tremely cold.

Knock, knock.
*Who's there?*
Eskimo Christmas.
*Eskimo Christmas who?*
Eskimo Christmas, I tell you no lies.

• • •

Knock, knock.
*Who's there?*
Megan, Elise, and Chicken.
*Megan, Elise, and Chicken who?*
"Megan, Elise—and Chicken it twice,
gonna find out who's naughty and nice."

• • •

Knock, knock.
*Who's there?*
Frostbite.
*Frostbite who?*
Frostbite your food, then chew it.

• • •

Knock, knock.
*Who's there?*
Value.
*Value who?*
Value be my Valentine?

Knock, knock.
*Who's there?*
Blue.
*Blue who?*
Blue your nose, the cold makes it run.

. . .

Knock, knock.
*Who's there?*
Summer.
*Summer who?*
Summer happier in hot weather,
others in cold.

. . .

Knock, knock.
*Who's there?*
Icy.
*Icy who?*
Icy a big polar bear over there.

. . .

Knock, knock.
*Who's there?*
Sleet.
*Sleet who?*
Sleet, I'm starving.

Knock, knock.
*Who's there?*
Icicle.
*Icicle who?*
Icicle down to the hardware and buy a snow
shovel.

• • •

Knock, knock.
*Who's there?*
Willoughby.
*Willoughby who?*
Willoughby my Valentine?

• • •

Knock, knock.
*Who's there?*
Sanitize.
*Sanitize who?*
Sanitize his reindeer to his sleigh.

• • •

Knock, knock.
*Who's there?*
Summertime.
*Summertime who?*
Summertime conscious—you're not!

Knock, knock.
*Who's there?*
Howard.
*Howard who?*
Howard you like to stand out in the cold—
    open the door!

• • •

Knock, knock.
*Who's there?*
Santa.
*Santa who?*
Santa forward on our team was ill today.

• • •

Knock, knock.
*Who's there?*
Irish.
*Irish who?*
"Irish you a Merry Christmas!"

• • •

Knock, knock.
*Who's there?*
Yule.
*Yule who?*
Yule hear from my lawyer about this.

Knock, knock.
*Who's there?*
Vision.
*Vision who?*
Vision you a Happy New Year!

. . .

Knock, knock.
*Who's there?*
Autumn.
*Autumn who?*
You autumn sleep in the wigwam tonight.

. . .

Knock, knock.
*Who's there?*
Windy.
*Windy who?*
Windy lottery and give a tithe to your
    church.

. . .

Knock, knock.
*Who's there?*
Energize.
*Energize who?*
Her hair is blond, energize are blue.

Knock, knock.
*Who's there?*
Churchill.
*Churchill who?*
Churchill be the best place for a summer
    wedding.

•  •  •

Knock, knock.
*Who's there?*
Aloha.
*Aloha who?*
"Aloha myself down the chimney," says
                Santa.

•  •  •

Knock, knock.
*Who's there?*
Weather.
*Weather who?*
You tell me weather it will rain or not.

•  •  •

Knock, knock.
*Who's there?*
Easter.
*Easter who?*
Easter anybody at home?

Knock, knock.
*Who's there?*
Spring.
*Spring who?*
My yo-yo spring has a knot in it.

• • •

Knock, knock.
*Who's there?*
November.
*November who?*
November last Thanksgiving? Yum!

• • •

Knock, knock.
*Who's there?*
Gladys.
*Gladys who?*
Gladys Valentine's Day.

• • •

Knock, knock.
*Who's there?*
New year!
*New year who?*
New year were gonna ask me that.

# THE OTHER GIRLS

Knock, knock.
*Who's there?*
Lena.
*Lena who?*
Lena little closer and I'll tell you a secret.

. . .

Knock, knock.
*Who's there?*
Jen.
*Jen who?*
Jen in Rome, do as the Romans do.

Knock, knock.
*Who's there?*
Beth.
*Beth who?*
Beth wishes, thweetie!

• • •

Knock, knock.
*Who's there?*
Flo.
*Flo who?*
Flo-ride is good for your teeth.

• • •

Knock, knock.
*Who's there?*
Emma.
*Emma who?*
Emma gonna have to knock again, or are
    you gonna open this door?

• • •

Knock, knock.
*Who's there?*
Carol.
*Carol who?*
Carol go if you switch on the ignition.

Knock, knock.
*Who's there?*
Fanny.
*Fanny who?*
Fanny the way you keep saying "Who's there?" when I knock.

• • •

Knock, knock.
*Who's there?*
Lucy.
*Lucy who?*
I Lucy my keysie, open the doorsie.

• • •

Knock, knock.
*Who's there?*
Danielle.
*Danielle who?*
Danielle at me, please!

• • •

Knock, knock.
*Who's there?*
Minnie.
*Minnie who?*
Minnie hands make light work.

Knock, knock.
*Who's there?*
Emma.
*Emma who?*
Emma new neighbor. Nice to meet you.

• • •

Knock, knock.
*Who's there?*
Germaine.
*Germaine who?*
Germaine you don't recognize my voice?

• • •

Knock, knock.
*Who's there?*
Barbara.
*Barbara who?*
Barbara black sheep.

• • •

Knock, knock.
*Who's there?*
Viola.
*Viola who?*
Viola fuss? I'm not late.

Knock, knock.
*Who's there?*
Emma.
*Emma who?*
Emma bit cold out here. Let me in!

•  •  •

Knock, knock.
*Who's there?*
Marjorie.
*Marjorie who?*
Marjorie found me guilty, now I'm in jail.

•  •  •

Knock, knock.
*Who's there?*
Eileen.
*Eileen who?*
Eileen too hard on this door and it'll break.
Let me in!

•  •  •

Knock, knock.
*Who's there?*
Candice.
*Candice who?*
Candice be true love at long last?

Knock, knock.
*Who's there?*
Gwen.
*Gwen who?*
Gwen it rains, it pours.

• • •

Knock, knock.
*Who's there?*
Sadie.
*Sadie who?*
Sadie Pledge of Allegiance to the flag.

• • •

Knock, knock.
*Who's there?*
Mabel.
*Mabel who?*
Mabel doesn't ring either.

• • •

Knock, knock.
*Who's there?*
Lass.
*Lass who?*
That's what cowboys use, isn't it?

Knock, knock.
*Who's there?*
Ima.
*Ima who?*
"Ima wondering wreck from Georgia Tech."

• • •

Knock, knock.
*Who's there?*
Mary.
*Mary who?*
Mary me at once, my darling!

• • •

Knock, knock.
*Who's there?*
Wanda Way.
*Wanda Way who?*
Wanda Way, and you'll get lost.

• • •

Knock, knock.
*Who's there?*
Candace.
*Candace who?*
Candace be the last knock-knock joke?
(NO!)

Knock, knock.
*Who's there?*
Rita.
*Rita who?*
Rita book, instead of these dumb knock-
knock jokes.

. . .

Knock, knock.
*Who's there?*
Amanda.
*Amanda who?*
Amanda fix your TV set.

. . .

Knock, knock.
*Who's there?*
Dee.
*Dee who?*
Dee-livery. Your pizza's getting cold.

. . .

Knock, knock.
*Who's there?*
Laura.
*Laura who?*
Laura the blinds, the sun's too bright.

Knock, knock.
*Who's there?*
Selma.
*Selma who?*
Selma shares in the company. Stock's going
south.

• • •

Knock, knock.
*Who's there?*
Robin.
*Robin who?*
Robin banks is not a very good profession.

• • •

Knock, knock.
*Who's there?*
Yvonne.
*Yvonne who?*
Yvonne to know how to play soccer?

• • •

Knock, knock.
*Who's there?*
Harriet.
*Harriet who?*
Harriet too much. There's none for me.

Knock, knock.
*Who's there?*
Elsie.
*Elsie who?*
Elsie you later.

. . .

Knock, knock.
*Who's there?*
Henrietta.
*Henrietta who?*
Henrietta grasshopper!

. . .

Knock, knock.
*Who's there?*
I, Irma.
*I, Irma who?*
I, Irma keep by working hard.

. . .

Knock, knock.
*Who's there?*
Phyllis.
*Phyllis who?*
Phyllis in on the latest news.

Knock, knock.
*Who's there?*
Rita.
*Rita who?*
Rita good book lately?

• • •

Knock, knock.
*Who's there?*
Ida.
*Ida who?*
Ida called you first, but my phone is dead.

• • •

Knock, knock.
*Who's there?*
Thea.
*Thea who?*
Thea later, alligator.

• • •

Knock, knock.
*Who's there?*
Wilma.
*Wilma who?*
Wilma lunch be ready soon?

Knock, knock.
*Who's there?*
Gladys.
*Gladys who?*
Gladys Friday?

. . .

Knock, knock.
*Who's there?*
Sharon.
*Sharon who?*
Sharon share alike.

. . .

Knock, knock.
*Who's there?*
A little girl.
*A little girl who?*
A little girl who can't reach the doorbell!

. . .

Knock, knock.
*Who's there?*
Doris.
*Doris who?*
Doris open, come on in!

Knock, knock.
*Who's there?*
Doris.
*Doris who?*
Doris closed, that's why I'm knocking.

• • •

Knock, knock.
*Who's there?*
Danielle.
*Danielle who?*
Danielle, I can hear you.

• • •

Knock, knock.
*Who's there?*
Sara.
*Sara who?*
Sara doctor in the house?

• • •

Knock, knock.
*Who's there?*
Isabelle.
*Isabelle who?*
Isabelle necessary on the door?

# THE ANIMAL FARE

Knock, knock.
*Who's there?*
Goat.
*Goat who?*
Goat to the door and find out!

. . .

Knock, knock.
*Who's there?*
Bat.
*Bat who?*
Bat you can't wait to read the next one.

Knock, knock.
*Who's there?*
Goosie.
*Goosie who?*
Goosie who's at the door.

. . .

Knock, knock.
*Who's there?*
Chocolate chirp.
*Chocolate chirp who?*
Birds eat Chocolate chirp cookies.

. . .

Knock, knock.
*Who's there?*
Lambulance.
*Lambulance who?*
Lambulance took baby sheep to the hospital.

. . .

Knock, knock.
*Who's there?*
Gopher.
*Gopher who?*
Gopher the gold!

Knock, knock.
*Who's there?*
Flea.
*Flea who?*
Flea blind mice.

• • •

Knock, knock.
*Who's there?*
Wallabee.
*Wallabee who?*
Wallabee sting more than once?

• • •

Knock, knock.
*Who's there?*
Buck.
*Buck who?*
Buck, buck, I'm a chicken.

• • •

Knock, knock.
*Who's there?*
Gopher.
*Gopher who?*
Gopher a nice swim.

Knock, knock.
*Who's there?*
Mary Hannah.
*Mary Hannah who?*
Mary Hannah little lamb.

. . .

Knock, knock.
*Who's there?*
Gnu.
*Gnu who?*
Gnu Zealand is a cool place to visit.

. . .

Knock, knock.
*Who's there?*
Cows go.
*Cows go who?*
No silly, cows go MOOO!

. . .

Knock, knock.
*Who's there?*
Oink, oink.
*Oink, oink who?*
Make up your mind if you're going to be a
pig or an owl.

Knock, knock.
*Who's there?*
Tuna.
*Tuna who?*
You can tuna piano, but you can't tuna fish.

• • •

Knock, knock.
*Who's there?*
Chimney.
*Chimney who?*
Chimney cricket!

• • •

Knock, knock.
*Who's there?*
Donna.
*Donna who?*
Donna put the cart before the horse.

• • •

Knock, knock.
*Who's there?*
Bow.
*Bow who?*
Not bow who, bow wow!

Knock, knock.
*Who's there?*
Tick.
*Tick who?*
Tick 'em up. I'm a tig, tad, towboy!

• • •

Knock, knock.
*Who's there?*
Duck.
*Duck who?*
Just duck! They're throwing stuff at us!

• • •

Knock, knock.
*Who's there?*
Spider.
*Spider who?*
You tried to hide her, but I spider.

• • •

Knock, knock.
*Who's there?*
Gorilla.
*Gorilla who?*
Gorilla me a burger, please.

Knock, knock.
*Who's there?*
Easter.
*Easter who?*
The Easter Bunny.

• • •

Knock, knock.
*Who's there?*
Anna.
*Anna who?*
Anna-nother Easter Bunny.

• • •

Knock, knock.
*Who's there?*
Moira.
*Moira who?*
Moira Easter Bunnies.

• • •

Knock, knock.
*Who's there?*
Howie.
*Howie who?*
Howie gonna get rid of all these Easter
Bunnies?

Knock, knock.
*Who's there?*
Pig.
*Pig who?*
Pig up your feet or you'll twip!

• • •

Knock, knock.
*Who's there?*
Zookeeper.
*Zookeeper who?*
Zookeeper shirt on!

• • •

Knock, knock.
*Who's there?*
Alpaca.
*Alpaca who?*
Alpaca the trunk, while you pack the
    suitcase.

• • •

Knock, knock.
*Who's there?*
Owls.
*Owls who?*
I know that!

Knock, knock.
*Who's there?*
Robin.
*Robin who?*
Robin is against the law.

. . .

Knock, knock.
*Who's there?*
Owl.
*Owl who?*
Owl you know unless you open the door?

. . .

Knock, knock.
*Who's there?*
Grr!
*Grr who?*
Are you a bear or an owl?

. . .

Knock, knock.
*Who's there?*
Rabbit.
*Rabbit who?*
Rabbit up pretty, it's for my girl.

Knock, knock.
*Who's there?*
Dinosaur.
*Dinosaur who?*
Dinosaur because he stubbed his toe.

• • •

Knock, knock.
*Who's there?*
Ocelot.
*Ocelot who?*
Ocelot of questions, don't you?

• • •

Knock, knock.
*Who's there?*
Whale.
*Whale who?*
Whale meet you at your house.

• • •

Knock, knock.
*Who's there?*
Panther.
*Panther who?*
Panther at the cleaners.

Knock, knock.
*Who's there?*
Llama.
*Llama who?*
Llama bit lost, point me the right way.

. . .

Knock, knock.
*Who's there?*
Lion.
*Lion who?*
I'm lion out here on your porch—open up!

. . .

Knock, knock.
*Who's there?*
Ketchup.
*Ketchup who?*
Is that ketchup the tree again?

. . .

Knock, knock.
*Who's there?*
Kanga.
*Kanga who?*
No, Kangaroo!

Knock, knock.
*Who's there?*
Gnats.
*Gnats who?*
Gnats not a laughing matter. Open this
    door!

. . .

Knock, knock.
*Who's there?*
Oily.
*Oily who?*
The oily bird catches the worm.

. . .

Knock, knock.
*Who's there?*
Owl.
*Owl who?*
Owl I can say is, "Knock, knock."

. . .

Knock, knock.
*Who's there?*
Lamb.
*Lamb who?*
"Don't lamb the door," his mom says.

Knock, knock.
*Who's there?*
Toucan.
*Toucan who?*
Toucan live as cheaply as one.

. . .

Knock, knock.
*Who's there?*
Willoughby.
*Whilloughby who?*
Willoughby a monkey's uncle!

. . .

Knock, knock.
*Who's there?*
Detail.
*Detail who?*
Detail is wagging the dog.

. . .

Knock, knock.
*Who's there?*
Chicken Poodle.
*Chicken Poodle who?*
Chicken Poodle is my pups favorite soup.

Knock, knock.
*Who's there?*
Beagle.
*Beagle who?*
Beagle with cream cheese.

. . .

Knock, knock.
*Who's there?*
Walrus.
*Walrus who?*
Why do you Walrus ask silly questions?

. . .

Knock, knock.
*Who's there?*
Flea.
*Flea who?*
Flea, flie, flo, flum!

. . .

Knock, knock.
*Who's there?*
Donkey.
*Donkey who?*
Donkey know that I want to be alone.

Knock, knock.
*Who's there?*
Dragon.
*Dragon who?*
Dragon out of here you slowpoke.

. . .

Knock, knock.
*Who's there?*
Puss.
*Puss who?*
Puss the gate shut when you leave.

. . .

Knock, knock.
*Who's there?*
Cattle.
*Cattle who?*
The cattle drive you crazy.

. . .

Knock, knock.
*Who's there?*
Possom.
*Possom who?*
Possom the salt, please.

Knock, knock.
*Who's there?*
Owl.
*Owl who?*
Owl tell you one of these days.

• • •

Knock, knock.
*Who's there?*
Walter.
*Walter who?*
Walter off a duck's back.

• • •

Knock, knock.
*Who's there?*
Bear.
*Bear who?*
Please bear with me, I want some honey.

• • •

Knock, knock.
*Who's there?*
Cheese.
*Cheese who?*
Cheese the cheetah of my dreams.

# JUKE BOX RAPPIN'

Knock, knock.
*Who's there?*
Wendy.
*Wendy who?*
"Wendy red red robin come bob bob bob-
bing along."

. . .

Knock, knock.
*Who's there?*
Yachts.
*Yachts who?*
"Yachts new pussycat?"

Knock, knock.
*Who's there?*
Olive carrots.
*Olive carrots who?*
"Olive carrots in the summertime; Olive
    carrots in the fall."

• • •

Knock, knock.
*Who's there?*
Mustard.
*Mustard who?*
"You Mustard been a beautiful baby."

• • •

Knock, knock.
*Who's there?*
Kimona.
*Kimona who?*
"Kimona my house, my house come on."

• • •

Knock, knock.
*Who's there?*
Omar.
*Omar who?*
"Omar darling Clementine."

Knock, knock.
*Who's there?*
Mayonnaise.
*Mayonnaise who?*
"Mayonnaise have seen the glory of the
   coming of the Lord."

. . .

Knock, knock.
*Who's there?*
Zipper.
*Zipper who?*
"Zipper dee-doo-dah!"

. . .

Knock, knock.
*Who's there?*
Levin.
*Levin who?*
"Levin on a jet plane."

. . .

Knock, knock.
*Who's there?*
Sombrero.
*Sombrero who?*
"Sombrero-ver the rainbow."

Knock, knock.
*Who's there?*
Butcher.
*Butcher who?*
"Butcher arms around me baby, hold me
   tight."

. . .

Knock, knock.
*Who's there?*
Olive.
*Olive who?*
"Olive me, why not take olive me?"

. . .

Knock, knock.
*Who's there?*
Wendy.
*Wendy who?*
"Wendy wind blows, the cradle will rock."

. . .

Knock, knock.
*Who's there?*
Abysinnia.
*Abysinnia who?*
"Abysinnia in all the old familiar places."

Knock, knock.
*Who's there?*
Andy Green.
*Andy Green who?*
"Andy Green grass grows all around, all around."

· · ·

Knock, knock.
*Who's there?*
Toast.
*Toast who?*
"Toast were the days my friends."

· · ·

Knock, knock.
*Who's there?*
Weasel.
*Weasel who?*
"Weasel while you work."

· · ·

Knock, knock.
*Who's there?*
Crimea.
*Crimea who?*
"I'm gonna Crimea river."

Knock, knock.
*Who's there?*
Oil.
*Oil who?*
"Oil be seeing you, in all the old familiar
   places."

.   .   .

Knock, knock.
*Who's there?*
Barton.
*Barton who?*
"Barton up your overcoat."

.   .   .

Knock, knock.
*Who's there?*
Demons.
*Demons who?*
"Demons are a ghoul's best friend."

.   .   .

Knock, knock.
*Who's there?*
Caesar.
*Caesar who?*
"Caesar jolly good fellow."

Knock, knock.
*Who's there?*
Ice Cream.
*Ice Cream who?*
"Ice Cream of Jeannie with the light brown
hair."

. . .

Knock, knock.
*Who's there?*
Domino.
*Domino who?*
"Domino thing if you ain't got that swing."

. . .

Knock, knock.
*Who's there?*
Apocryphal.
*Apocryphal who?*
"Apocryphal full of dreams."

. . .

Knock, knock.
*Who's there?*
Dexter.
*Dexter who?*
"Dexter halls with boughs of holly."

Knock, knock.
*Who's there?*
Bay.
*Bay who?*
"Bay-by face, you've got the sweetest little
baby face."

. . .

Knock, knock.
*Who's there?*
Yule.
*Yule who?*
"Yule never know just how much I love you."

. . .

Knock, knock.
*Who's there?*
Barry.
*Barry who?*
"Oh Barry me not, on the lone prairie."

. . .

Knock, knock.
*Who's there?*
Snow.
*Snow who?*
"There's snow business like show business."

Knock, knock.
*Who's there?*
Sonia.
*Sonia who?*
"Sonia a paper moon."

. . .

Knock, knock.
*Who's there?*
Terry.
*Terry who?*
"Terry's nothing like a dame."

. . .

Knock, knock.
*Who's there?*
Annie.
*Annie who?*
"Annie thing you can do, I can do better."

. . .

Knock, knock.
*Who's there?*
Ooze.
*Ooze who?*
"Ooze that knocking at my door?"

Knock, knock.
*Who's there?*
Joel.
*Joel who?*
"Joel MacDonald had a farm."

• • •

Knock, knock.
*Who's there?*
Snake.
*Snake who?*
"Snake me out to the ballgame."

• • •

Knock, knock.
*Who's there?*
Hopi.
*Hopi who?*
"Hopi days are here again."

• • •

Knock, knock.
*Who's there?*
Toothache.
*Toothache who?*
"Toothache the high road and I'll take the
low road. . ."

Knock, knock.
*Who's there?*
Gnome.
*Gnome who?*
"Gnome sweet gnome."

• • •

Knock, knock.
*Who's there?*
Rupert.
*Rupert who?*
"Rupert your left arm in, and your left arm
out. . ."

• • •

Knock, knock.
*Who's there?*
Rocky.
*Rocky who?*
"Rocky-bye baby, on the tree top."

• • •

Knock, knock.
*Who's there?*
Aardvark.
*Aardvark who?*
"Aardvark a million miles for one of your
smiles."

# YUM
# A LA
# MODE

Knock, knock.
*Who's there?*
Turnip.
*Turnip who?*
Turnip the radio, please!

. . .

Knock, knock.
*Who's there?*
Cook.
*Cook who?*
What d'ya think you are—a clock?

Knock, knock.
*Who's there?*
Ketchup.
*Ketchup who?*
Ketchup to me and I'll tell you.

• • •

Knock, knock.
*Who's there?*
Oswald.
*Oswald who?*
Oswald my gum.

• • •

Knock, knock.
*Who's there?*
Cash.
*Cash who?*
No thanks, I prefer peanuts.

• • •

Knock, knock.
*Who's there?*
Broccoli.
*Broccoli who?*
Broccoli doesn't have a last name, silly!

Knock, knock.
*Who's there?*
Water.
*Water who?*
Water you doin' at my front door?

• • •

Knock, knock.
*Who's there?*
Water.
*Water who?*
Water way to answer the door.

• • •

Knock, knock.
*Who's there?*
Water.
*Water who?*
Water be ashamed of yourself, acting like
   that!

• • •

Knock, knock.
*Who's there?*
Bacon.
*Bacon who?*
I bacon your pardon!

Knock, knock.
*Who's there?*
Beagles.
*Beagles who?*
I'll have beagles and cream cheese.

• • •

Knock, knock.
*Who's there?*
Butcher.
*Butcher who?*
Butcher your money where your mouth is.

• • •

Knock, knock.
*Who's there?*
Effie.
*Effie who?*
Effie known you were coming, he'da baked
   a cake.

• • •

Knock, knock.
*Who's there?*
Beets.
*Beets who?*
Beets me, I forgot my name.

Knock, knock.
*Who's there?*
Bean.
*Bean who?*
Bean knocking so long my hand hurts.

. . .

Knock, knock.
*Who's there?*
I-8.
*I-8 who?*
I-8 lunch already. Is dinner ready?

. . .

Knock, knock.
*Who's there?*
Pecan.
*Pecan who?*
Pecan someone your own size.

. . .

Knock, knock.
*Who's there?*
Quiche.
*Quiche who?*
Quiche me, you big lug you.

Knock, knock.
*Who's there?*
Watson.
*Watson who?*
Watson the menu today?

• • •

Knock, knock.
*Who's there?*
Bacon.
*Bacon who?*
I'm bacon a cake for your birthday.

• • •

Knock, knock.
*Who's there?*
Window.
*Window who?*
Window we eat?

• • •

Knock, knock.
*Who's there?*
Viper.
*Viper who?*
Viper hands, they're sticky from
the chocolate.

Knock, knock.
*Who's there?*
Four eggs.
*Four eggs who?*
Four eggs ample.

. . .

Knock, knock.
*Who's there?*
Figs.
*Figs who?*
Figs the doorbell, it's broken.

. . .

Knock, knock.
*Who's there?*
Banana.
*Banana who?*
Banana split so ice creamed!

. . .

Knock, knock.
*Who's there?*
Apple.
*Apple who?*
Apple your hair if you don't open up!

Knock, knock.
*Who's there?*
Veal chop.
*Veal chop who?*
Veal chop around and find a bargain.

• • •

Knock, knock.
*Who's there?*
Renata.
*Renata who?*
Renata milk, may I borrow some?

• • •

Knock, knock.
*Who's there?*
Rice.
*Rice who?*
Rice and shine, sleepyhead!

• • •

Knock, knock.
*Who's there?*
Egg.
*Egg who?*
Egg-stremely cold out here!

Knock, knock.
*Who's there?*
Egg.
*Egg who?*
Egg-citing to meet you!

• • •

Knock, knock.
*Who's there?*
Cranberry.
*Cranberry who?*
Cranberry sleep over tonight?

• • •

Knock, knock.
*Who's there?*
Hammond.
*Hammond who?*
Hammond eggs for breakfast.

• • •

Knock, knock.
*Who's there?*
Orange juice.
*Orange juice who?*
Orange juice sorry you asked?

Knock, knock.
*Who's there?*
Orange juice.
*Orange juice who?*
Orange juice gonna talk to me?

• • •

Knock, knock.
*Who's there?*
Pizza Tut.
*Pizza Tut who?*
Pizza Tut, where mummies eat.

• • •

Knock, knock.
*Who's there?*
French flies.
*French flies who?*
Spider's love French flies.

• • •

Knock, knock.
*Who's there?*
Coal slaw.
*Coal slaw who?*
Coal slaw is a miner's food.

Knock, knock.
*Who's there?*
Hansel and Gristle.
*Hansel and Gristle who?*
Hansel and Gristle, a hamburger's favorite
    fairy tale.

• • •

Knock, knock.
*Who's there?*
Walnuts.
*Walnuts who?*
Walnuts around here—including me!

• • •

Knock, knock.
*Who's there?*
Artichoke.
*Artichoke who?*
Don't artichoke on a fish bone!

• • •

Knock, knock.
*Who's there?*
Asparagus.
*Asparagus who?*
Asparagus the gory details.

Knock, knock.
*Who's there?*
Yogurt.
*Yogurt who?*
Yogurt—look how well she runs!

. . .

Knock, knock.
*Who's there?*
Cottage cheese.
*Cottage cheese who?*
Cottage cheese thief in the cooler.

. . .

Knock, knock.
*Who's there?*
Lettuce.
*Lettuce who?*
Lettuce dig in and eat.

. . .

Knock, knock.
*Who's there?*
Cocoa.
*Cocoa who?*
The cocoa clock says it's noon.

# LOCKER KNOCKER

Knock, knock.
*Who's there?*
Water skier.
*Water skier who?*
Water skier'd of, I'm harmless!

• • •

Knock, knock.
*Who's there?*
Thermos.
*Thermos who?*
Thermos be someone home, I see a light on.

Knock, knock.
*Who's there?*
Short-slop.
*Short-slop who?*
Pigs play short-slop in baseball.

• • •

Knock, knock.
*Who's there?*
Stopwatch.
*Stopwatch who?*
Stopwatch you're doing.

• • •

Knock, knock.
*Who's there?*
Bat.
*Bat who?*
Bat you can't wait to read the next one.

• • •

Knock, knock.
*Who's there?*
Aikido.
*Aikido who?*
Aikido you not.

Knock, knock.
*Who's there?*
Howard.
*Howard who?*
Howard you like to play shortstop?

• • •

Knock, knock.
*Who's there?*
Datson.
*Datson who?*
Datson of mind can really play ball.

• • •

Knock, knock.
*Who's there?*
Kung flu.
*Kung flu who?*
Kung flu, a martial arts sickness.

• • •

Knock, knock.
*Who's there?*
Canada.
*Canada who?*
Canada boys come over to shoot hoops?

Knock, knock.
*Who's there?*
Walker.
*Walker who?*
Walker run—which shall we do?

• • •

Knock, knock.
*Who's there?*
Rhonda.
*Rhonda who?*
I'm going to Rhonda marathon.

• • •

Knock, knock.
*Who's there?*
Polo.
*Polo who?*
Polo the leader.

• • •

Knock, knock.
*Who's there?*
Thor.
*Thor who?*
Thor out!

Knock, knock.
*Who's there?*
Hedda.
*Hedda who?*
Hedda the pack.

• • •

Knock, knock.
*Who's there?*
Rose.
*Rose who?*
"Rose, Rose, Rose your boat. . ."

• • •

Knock, knock.
*Who's there?*
Nuisance.
*Nuisance who?*
What's nuisance yesterday.

• • •

Knock, knock.
*Who's there?*
Sarah.
*Sarah who?*
Sarah a florist in the house?

Knock, knock.
*Who's there?*
Quarterback.
*Quarterback who?*
Quarterback, or is it my tip?

. . .

Knock, knock.
*Who's there?*
Fizz-Ed.
*Fizz-Ed who?*
Fizz-Ed, a soda pop's favorite class.

. . .

Knock, knock.
*Who's there?*
Snow.
*Snow who?*
Snow ice skating today.

. . .

Knock, knock.
*Who's there?*
Pitcher.
*Pitcher who?*
Pitcher arms around me!

Knock, knock.
*Who's there?*
Willy.
*Willy who?*
Willy he make it? The crowds are sure for
   him!

· · ·

Knock, knock.
*Who's there?*
Tango.
*Tango who?*
Tango faster than you can.

· · ·

Knock, knock.
*Who's there?*
Coburn.
*Coburn who?*
Coburn your socks, they smell terrible.

· · ·

Knock, knock.
*Who's there?*
Tennis.
*Tennis who?*
Tennis more than six!

Knock, knock.
*Who's there?*
Tennis.
*Tennis who?*
What did tennis see?

• • •

Knock, knock.
*Who's there?*
Sally.
*Sally who?*
Sally-brate the Met's win!

• • •

Knock, knock.
*Who's there?*
Shoes.
*Shoes who?*
Shoes me, I didn't mean to steal second.

• • •

Knock, knock.
*Who's there?*
Tennis.
*Tennis who?*
Tennis the number that comes after nine.

Knock, knock.
*Who's there?*
Yukon.
*Yukon who?*
Yukon lead a slow horse to water, but you
can't make him drink.

• • •

Knock, knock.
*Who's there?*
Dennis.
*Dennis who?*
Dennis anyone?

• • •

Knock, knock.
*Who's there?*
Summer.
*Summer who?*
Summer good players, others are better.

• • •

Knock, knock.
*Who's there?*
Shelley.
*Shelley who?*
Shelley have a game of tennis?

Knock, knock.
*Who's there?*
Ron.
*Ron who?*
Ron, Ron, Ron as fast as you can—you can't catch me, I'm the gingerbread man!

. . .

Knock, knock.
*Who's there?*
Racket.
*Racket who?*
What's all the racket about?

. . .

Knock, knock.
*Who's there?*
Iris.
*Iris who?*
Iris-ked my life on the trampoline.

. . .

Knock, knock.
*Who's there?*
Darwin.
*Darwin who?*
Darwin-ning the game two to one!

Knock, knock.
*Who's there?*
Sara.
*Sara who?*
Sara doctor in the stadium?

• • •

Knock, knock.
*Who's there?*
Moose.
*Moose who?*
Moose likely Jen will win the hurdles.

• • •

Knock, knock.
*Who's there?*
Kip.
*Kip who?*
Kip your eyes on the goal.

• • •

Knock, knock.
*Who's there?*
Ethan.
*Ethan who?*
Ethan an apple a day keeps the
team doctor away.

Knock, knock.
*Who's there?*
Pancho.
*Pancho who?*
A pancho bag is used in a gym.

• • •

Knock, knock.
*Who's there?*
Yacht.
*Yacht who?*
Yacht to know me by now.

• • •

Knock, knock.
*Who's there?*
Lotta.
*Lotta who?*
Whole lotta-fouling in this game.

• • •

Knock, knock.
*Who's there?*
Kent.
*Kent who?*
Umpire kent see without his glasses.

Knock, knock.
*Who's there?*
Wayne.
*Wayne who?*
Wayne the going gets tough, the wrestlers
    get going.

. . .

Knock, knock.
*Who's there?*
Grant.
*Grant who?*
Losers grant and bear it.

. . .

Knock, knock.
*Who's there?*
Ghoulie.
*Ghoulie who?*
I play ghoulie on the monster team.

. . .

Knock, knock.
*Who's there?*
Gympanzee.
*Gympanzee who?*
The animal who lives in the gym.

Knock, knock.
*Who's there?*
Swum.
*Swum who?*
Swum of my best friends are horses.

• • •

Knock, knock.
*Who's there?*
Adolph.
*Adolph who?*
Adolph ball hit me on the head.

• • •

Knock, knock.
*Who's there?*
Basis.
*Basis who?*
Basis loaded, nobody out!

• • •

Knock, knock.
*Who's there?*
Judo.
*Judo who?*
So, what judo know?

Knock, knock.
*Who's there?*
Monroe.
*Monroe who?*
"Monroe, row, row, your boat. . ."

• • •

Knock, knock.
*Who's there?*
Lass.
*Lass who?*
Lass one in the pool is a rotten egg!

• • •

Knock, knock.
*Who's there?*
Andy.
*Andy who?*
Andy hit the ball over the right field fence.

• • •

Knock, knock.
*Who's there?*
Felon.
*Felon who?*
Felon on the hockey rink ice.

# HEAR SAY

Knock, knock.
*Who's there?*
Rook.
*Rook who?*
Rook out—the sky is falling!

. . .

Knock, knock.
*Who's there?*
Waiter.
*Waiter who?*
Waiter I get my hands on you!

Knock, knock.
*Who's there?*
Gruesome.
*Gruesome who?*
Gruesome, four inches.

• • •

Knock, knock.
*Who's there?*
Pilot.
*Pilot who?*
In my office I pilot of papers here, and I
pilot of papers there.

• • •

Knock, knock.
*Who's there?*
Miniature.
*Miniature who?*
Miniature open this door, I'll tell you.

• • •

Knock, knock.
*Who's there?*
Surreal.
*Surreal who?*
Surreal pleasure to meet you.

Knock, knock.
*Who's there?*
Wheelbarrow.
*Wheelbarrow who?*
Wheelbarrow some money for a holiday in
    Mexico.

• • •

Knock, knock.
*Who's there?*
Thumb.
*Thumb who?*
Thumb like it hot and thumb like it cold.

• • •

Knock, knock.
*Who's there?*
Queen.
*Queen who?*
Make your room as queen as a whistle.

• • •

Knock, knock.
*Who's there?*
Hair combs.
*Hair combs who?*
Hair combs the judge!

Knock, knock.
*Who's there?*
Lemon juice.
*Lemon juice who?*
Lemon juice you to my friend.

• • •

Knock, knock.
*Who's there?*
Waiter.
*Waiter who?*
Waiter sec while I tie my shoe.

• • •

Knock, knock.
*Who's there?*
Stopwatch.
*Stopwatch who?*
Stopwatch you're doing and open this door!

• • •

Knock, knock.
*Who's there?*
Nettie.
*Nettie who?*
Nettie as a fruitcake!

Knock, knock.
*Who's there?*
State Highway Patrol.
*State Highway Patrol who?*
Better not ask questions!

. . .

Knock, knock.
*Who's there?*
Hero.
*Hero who?*
Hero today, gone tomorrow.

. . .

Knock, knock.
*Who's there?*
Sacha.
*Sacha who?*
Sacha big fuss, just because I knocked on
    your door.

. . .

Knock, knock.
*Who's there?*
Theresa.
*Theresa who?*
Theresa fly in my soup.

Knock, knock.
*Who's there?*
Mandy.
*Mandy who?*
Mandy life boats, the boat is sinking!

• • •

Knock, knock.
*Who's there?*
Wendy.
*Wendy who?*
Wendy today, sunny tomorrow.

• • •

Knock, knock.
*Who's there?*
Harmony.
*Harmony who?*
Harmony times do I have to knock?

• • •

Knock, knock.
*Who's there?*
Anka.
*Anka who?*
Anka the boat.

Knock, knock.
*Who's there?*
Ten.
*Ten who?*
Ten to your own business, please!

• • •

Knock, knock.
*Who's there?*
Allied.
*Allied who?*
Allied, so sue me!

• • •

Knock, knock.
*Who's there?*
Wanda.
*Wanda who?*
Wanda make something out of it?

• • •

Knock, knock.
*Who's there?*
Hopi.
*Hopi who?*
Hopi quiet!

Knock, knock.
*Who's there?*
Censure.
*Censure who?*
Censure so smart, why aren't you rich?

• • •

Knock, knock.
*Who's there?*
Avoid.
*Avoid who?*
Avoid to the wise is sufficient.

• • •

Knock, knock.
*Who's there?*
Gut.
*Gut who?*
Cat gut your tongue?

• • •

Knock, knock.
*Who's there?*
Sneazy.
*Sneazy who?*
Sneazy as pie!

Knock, knock.
*Who's there?*
Avenue.
*Avenue who?*
Avenue been at my door before?

. . .

Knock, knock.
*Who's there?*
Luck.
*Luck who?*
Luck through the key hole and you'll find
out.

. . .

Knock, knock.
*Who's there?*
K-2.
*K-2 who?*
K-2 come in?

. . .

Knock, knock.
*Who's there?*
Ammonia.
*Ammonia who?*
Ammonia little girl.

Knock, knock.
*Who's there?*
Black panther.
*Black panther who?*
Black panther what I'm wearing. What
about you?

• • •

Knock, knock.
*Who's there?*
Kleenex.
*Kleenex who?*
Kleenex are better than dirty ones.

• • •

Knock, knock.
*Who's there?*
Wooden shoe.
*Wooden shoe who?*
Wooden shoe like an ice cream soda?

• • •

Knock, knock.
*Who's there?*
Titan.
*Titan who?*
Always titan your seat belt.

Knock, knock.
*Who's there?*
Ticket.
*Ticket who?*
I say, ticket or leave it.

• • •

Knock, knock.
*Who's there?*
Alpha.
*Alpha who?*
Alpha one, and one for all.

• • •

Knock, knock.
*Who's there?*
Waddle.
*Waddle who?*
Waddle you give me if I stop telling these
jokes?

• • •

Knock, knock.
*Who's there?*
Voodoo.
*Voodoo who?*
Voodoo you think you are?

Knock, knock.
*Who's there?*
Quacker.
*Quacker who?*
Quacker another bad joke and I'm outta
    here!

• • •

Knock, knock.
*Who's there?*
Wicked.
*Wicked who?*
Wicked make beautiful music together.

• • •

Knock, knock.
*Who's there?*
Needle.
*Needle who?*
Needle the help I can get.

• • •

Knock, knock.
*Who's there?*
Hughes.
*Hughes who?*
Hughes cars aren't brand new.

# STATE & CITY LIMITS

Knock, knock.
*Who's there?*
Texas.
*Texas who?*
Texas are high in this city.

• • •

Knock, knock.
*Who's there?*
Amarillo.
*Amarillo who?*
Amarillo fashioned girl.

Knock, knock.
*Who's there?*
Colorado.
*Colorado who?*
Colorado any color you want.

· · ·

Knock, knock.
*Who's there?*
Aurora.
*Aurora who?*
Aurora is what a lion says.

· · ·

Knock, knock.
*Who's there?*
Dakota.
*Dakota who?*
Dakota fits fine, but the pants are too long.

· · ·

Knock, knock.
*Who's there?*
Huron.
*Huron who?*
Pardon me, but Huron my foot!

Knock, knock.
*Who's there?*
Arizona.
*Arizona who?*
Arizona room for one of us in this town.

• • •

Knock, knock.
*Who's there?*
Tucson.
*Tucson who?*
Tucson and two daughters are enough.

• • •

Knock, knock.
*Who's there?*
Navajo.
*Navajo who?*
You'll Navajo until you open the door.

• • •

Knock, knock.
*Who's there?*
Yuma.
*Yuma who?*
Yuma best friend.

Knock, knock.
*Who's there?*
California.
*California who?*
California on her phone yet?

. . .

Knock, knock.
*Who's there?*
Sierra.
*Sierra who?*
Sierra later, alligator!

. . .

Knock, knock.
*Who's there?*
Venice.
*Venice who?*
Venice payday? I'm broke.

. . .

Knock, knock.
*Who's there?*
New York.
*New York who?*
New York is the name of my new Yorkie.

Knock, knock.
*Who's there?*
Hackensack.
*Hackensack who?*
Hackensack it to ya.

• • •

Knock, knock.
*Who's there?*
Utica.
*Utica who?*
Utica the high road and
I'll take the low road.

• • •

Knock, knock.
*Who's there?*
Mass.
*Mass who?*
Mass is said at church in Massachusetts.

• • •

Knock, knock.
*Who's there?*
Nantucket.
*Nantucket who?*
Nantucket, but she'll have to give it back.

Knock, knock.
*Who's there?*
Oregon.
*Oregon who?*
Oregon is two chocolate cookies with white
   stuff in the middle.

. . .

Knock, knock.
*Who's there?*
Tacoma.
*Tacoma who?*
Tacoma your hair, it's a mess.

. . .

Knock, knock.
*Who's there?*
Utah.
*Utah who?*
Utah the puddy cat, too?

. . .

Knock, knock.
*Who's there?*
Idaho.
*Idaho who?*
Idaho-ed the whole garden if I had time.

Knock, knock.
*Who's there?*
Oregon.
*Oregon who?*
Is Oregon yet?

. . .

Knock, knock.
*Who's there?*
Tennessee.
*Tennessee who?*
Tennessee you tonight?

. . .

Knock, knock.
*Who's there?*
Delaware.
*Delaware who?*
Delaware a pretty dress to the ball.

. . .

Knock, knock.
*Who's there?*
Mississippi.
*Mississippi who?*
Mr. and Mississippi are in room one.

Knock, knock.
*Who's there?*
Missouri.
*Missouri who?*
Missouri loves company.

• • •

Knock, knock.
*Who's there?*
Hawaii.
*Hawaii who?*
I'm fine, Hawaii you?

• • •

Knock, knock.
*Who's there?*
Arkansas.
*Arkansas who?*
Arkansas through any piece of wood.

• • •

Knock, knock.
*Who's there?*
Kansas.
*Kansas who?*
Kansas be Friday already?

Knock, knock.
*Who's there?*
Dakota.
*Dakota who?*
Dakota is too heavy for this weather.

. . .

Knock, knock.
*Who's there?*
Alabama.
*Alabama who?*
Alabama and the 40 Thieves.

. . .

Knock, knock.
*Who's there?*
Maine.
*Maine who?*
Auntie Maine is really funny.

. . .

Knock, knock.
*Who's there?*
Washington.
*Washington who?*
Washingtons of laundry is hard work!

Knock, knock.
*Who's there?*
Maryland.
*Maryland who?*
Maryland owners, not poor men.

· · ·

Knock, knock.
*Who's there?*
Annapolis.
*Annapolis who?*
Annapolis red and round.

· · ·

Knock, knock.
*Who's there?*
Idaho.
*Idaho who?*
Did Idaho the bean patch?

· · ·

Knock, knock.
*Who's there?*
Michigan.
*Michigan who?*
"Michigan!" said the batter after the third
strike.

Knock, knock.
*Who's there?*
Georgia.
*Georgia who?*
Georgia the jungle, watch out for that tree!

• • •

Knock, knock.
*Who's there?*
Macon.
*Macon who?*
Macon a mountain out of a mole hill.

• • •

Knock, knock.
*Who's there?*
Wyoming.
*Wyoming who?*
Ever wonder Wyoming pigeons always
    return?

• • •

Knock, knock.
*Who's there?*
Alaska.
*Alaska who?*
Alaska my Mom if I can come over.

Knock, knock.
*Who's there?*
Yukon.
*Yukon who?*
"Yukon fool some of the people some of the
time. . ."

. . .

Knock, knock.
*Who's there?*
Juneau.
*Juneau who?*
No, I don't. Do you?

. . .

Knock, knock.
*Who's there?*
Eskimo.
*Eskimo who?*
Eskimo questions, I'll tell you no lies.

. . .

Knock, knock.
*Who's there?*
Lois.
*Lois who?*
Lois man on the totem pole.

Knock, knock.
*Who's there?*
Yukon.
*Yukon who?*
Yukon go your way, but I'll remember you.

•  •  •

Knock, knock.
*Who's there?*
Iowa.
*Iowa who?*
Iowa ten dollars; I'm here to pay.

•  •  •

Knock, knock.
*Who's there?*
Waterloo.
*Waterloo who?*
Waterloo doing after work tonight?

•  •  •

Knock, knock.
*Who's there?*
Newt.
*Newt who?*
Newt Jersey is the garden state.

Knock, knock.
*Who's there?*
Ohio.
*Ohio who?*
Ohio Silver!

• • •

Knock, knock.
*Who's there?*
Akron.
*Akron who?*
"Akron give you anything but love, baby."

• • •

Knock, knock.
*Who's there?*
Illinois.
*Illinois who?*
When you're sick, the sounds you make are
    Illinois.

• • •

Knock, knock.
*Who's there?*
Altoona.
*Altoona who?*
Altoona the piano if you'll sing.

Knock, knock.
*Who's there?*
Chuck.
*Chuck who?*
"Chuck-ago, Chuck-ago, that wonderful
    town."

• • •

Knock, knock.
*Who's there?*
Carrot.
*Carrot who?*
"Carrot me back to old Virginny."

• • •

Knock, knock.
*Who's there?*
Oklahoma.
*Oklahoma who?*
Oklahoma is OK!

# RAP
# THE MAP

Knock, knock.
*Who's there?*
Amazon.
*Amazon who?*
Amazon of a gun.

. . .

Knock, knock.
*Who's there?*
Kenya.
*Kenya who?*
Kenya give me a hand?

Knock, knock.
*Who's there?*
Budapest.
*Budapest who?*
You're nothing but a Budapest!

• • •

Knock, knock.
*Who's there?*
Samoa.
*Samoa who?*
Samoa coffee, please.

• • •

Knock, knock.
*Who's there?*
Philippians.
*Philippians who?*
Philippians do not come from the
    Philippines.

• • •

Knock, knock.
*Who's there?*
Manila.
*Manila who?*
Manila ice cream.

Knock, knock.
*Who's there?*
Italy.
*Italy who?*
Italy up the scores, and see who's won.

• • •

Knock, knock.
*Who's there?*
Pisa.
*Pisa who?*
Pepperoni pisa, that's who!

• • •

Knock, knock.
*Who's there?*
Venice.
*Venice who?*
Venice your mom coming home?

• • •

Knock, knock.
*Who's there?*
Uganda.
*Uganda who?*
Uganda come in without knocking.

Knock, knock.
*Who's there?*
Jamaica.
*Jamaica who?*
Jamaica me sick!

• • •

Knock, knock.
*Who's there?*
Armenia.
*Armenia who?*
Armenia every word I say.

• • •

Knock, knock.
*Who's there?*
Irish.
*Irish who?*
Irish I could carry a tune.

• • •

Knock, knock.
*Who's there?*
Siam.
*Siam who?*
Siam your old pal!

Knock, knock.
*Who's there?*
Siamese.
*Siamese who?*
Siamese-y to please.

. . .

Knock, knock.
*Who's there?*
Tibet.
*Tibet who?*
"Early Tibet, early to rise. . ."

. . .

Knock, knock.
*Who's there?*
Sahara.
*Sahara who?*
Sahara you dune?

. . .

Knock, knock.
*Who's there?*
Saturn.
*Saturn who?*
"This is Saturn-day Night Live!"

Knock, knock.
*Who's there?*
Island.
*Island who?*
Island on your roof with my parachute.

• • •

Knock, knock.
*Who's there?*
Uruguay.
*Uruguay who?*
You go Uruguay, and I'll go mine.

• • •

Knock, knock.
*Who's there?*
Taiwan.
*Taiwan who?*
Taiwan to be happy.

• • •

Knock, knock.
*Who's there?*
Uganda.
*Uganda who?*
Uganda get away with this!

Knock, knock.
*Who's there?*
Russia.
*Russia who?*
Russia large pizza to this address.

. . .

Knock, knock.
*Who's there?*
Moscow.
*Moscow who?*
Moscow gives more milk than Pa's cow.

. . .

Knock, knock.
*Who's there?*
Toronto.
*Toronto who?*
Toronto be a law against these knock-knock
   jokes.

. . .

Knock, knock.
*Who's there?*
Israel.
*Israel who?*
Israel, it's not a phony.

Knock, knock.
*Who's there?*
Irish.
*Irish who?*
Irish I had a thousand dollars.

• • •

Knock, knock.
*Who's there?*
Europe.
*Europe who?*
Europe'ning the door too slow. Let me in!

• • •

Knock, knock.
*Who's there?*
Formosa.
*Formosa who?*
Formosa the day I was home sick.

• • •

Knock, knock.
*Who's there?*
Aussie.
*Aussie who?*
Aussie you later, mate.

Knock, knock.
*Who's there?*
Sweden.
*Sweden who?*
Sweden the lemonade, it's sour.

• • •

Knock, knock.
*Who's there?*
Europa.
*Europa who?*
Europa steer and I'll watch.

• • •

Knock, knock.
*Who's there?*
Afghanistan.
*Afghanistan who?*
Afghanistan out here all day!

• • •

Knock, knock.
*Who's there?*
Far East.
*Far East who?*
"Far East a jolly good fellow. . ."

Knock, knock.
*Who's there?*
Norway.
*Norway who?*
Norway can you go out dressed like that!

. . .

Knock, knock.
*Who's there?*
Oslo.
*Oslo who?*
Oslo down, won't you?

. . .

Knock, knock.
*Who's there?*
Egypt.
*Egypt who?*
Egypt me! Call the police!

. . .

Knock, knock.
*Who's there?*
Cairo.
*Cairo who?*
Cairo the boat for a while?

Knock, knock.
*Who's there?*
China.
*China who?*
"China. Is there anyone fina, in the state of
    Carolina?"

• • •

Knock, knock.
*Who's there?*
Romania.
*Romania who?*
Romania-cs are great romancers.

• • •

Knock, knock.
*Who's there?*
Paris.
*Paris who?*
Paris me an apple, please.

• • •

Knock, knock.
*Who's there?*
Rome.
*Rome who?*
I'm ready to Rome home.

Knock, knock.
*Who's there?*
Hong Kong.
*Hong Kong who?*
Hong Kong did not climb the Empire State
   building.

• • •

Knock, knock.
*Who's there?*
Haiti.
*Haiti who?*
I Haiti, but coffee is fine.

• • •

Knock, knock.
*Who's there?*
Atlas.
*Atlas who?*
Atlas I'm home!

• • •

Knock, knock.
*Who's there?*
Trinidad.
*Trinidad who?*
Trinidad get better grades than his son?

Knock, knock.
*Who's there?*
Compass.
*Compass who?*
Compass the Coliseum, then turn right to
the Forum.

. . .

Knock, knock.
*Who's there?*
Panama.
*Panama who?*
Never Panama, or a pa.

. . .

Knock, knock.
*Who's there?*
Hungary.
*Hungary who?*
The maid Hungary's laundry on the line.

. . .

Knock, knock.
*Who's there?*
Turkey.
*Turkey who?*
Consider ham for Thanksgiving dinner!

# KITH 'N' KIN

Knock, knock.
*Who's there?*
Dad.
*Dad who?*
Dad fuel to the fire!

• • •

Knock, knock.
*Who's there?*
Yo momma.
*Yo momma who?*
I said, this is yo momma. So you better get
this door open!

Knock, knock.
*Who's there?*
Nadya.
*Nadya who?*
Nadya head if your understand.

· · ·

Knock, knock.
*Who's there?*
Granny.

Knock, knock.
*Who's there?*
Granny.

Knock, knock.
*Who's there?*
Granny.

Knock, knock.
*Who's there?*
Auntie.
*Auntie who?*
Auntie you getting sick of Granny?

Knock, knock.
*Who's there?*
Shutter.
*Shutter who?*
Shutter up, sis is talking too much!

• • •

Knock, knock.
*Who's there?*
Wooden.
*Wooden who?*
Wooden it be nice if Grandma were here?

• • •

Knock, knock.
*Who's there?*
Osborne.
*Osborne who?*
Osborne in the U.S.A.

• • •

Knock, knock.
*Who's there?*
Me.
*Me who?*
You don't know who you are yet?

Knock, knock.
*Who's there?*
Granny.
*Granny who?*
Granny me a minute of your time.

• • •

Knock, knock.
*Who's there?*
Your Dad!
*Your Dad who?*
Very funny, now let me in!

• • •

Knock, knock.
*Who's there?*
Your niece.
*Your niece who?*
Your niece to come home, to.

• • •

Knock, knock.
*Who's there?*
Colleen.
*Colleen who?*
Mom says Colleen up your room!

Knock, knock.
*Who's there?*
Denise.
*Denise who?*
Denise is de sister of de nephew.

• • •

Knock, knock.
*Who's there?*
Ma Bell.
*Ma Bell who?*
Ma Bell is out of order—knock!

• • •

Knock, knock.
*Who's there?*
Mama San.
*Mama San who?*
Mama San the warpath!

• • •

Knock, knock.
*Who's there?*
Creature.
*Creature who?*
Creature sibling with respect!

Knock, knock.
*Who's there?*
Vera.
*Vera who?*
Vera dad's cupcakes?

. . .

Knock, knock.
*Who's there?*
Isabell.
*Isabell who?*
Grandpa, Isabell necessary for my bike?

. . .

Knock, knock.
*Who's there?*
Thelma.
*Thelma who?*
Thelma I went out for pizza.

. . .

Knock, knock.
*Who's there?*
Auntie.
*Auntie who?*
Auntie will be served, along with watercress
sandwiches.

Knock, knock.
*Who's there?*
Waiter.
*Waiter who?*
Waiter I get my hands on you, cuz!

· · ·

Knock, knock.
*Who's there?*
Step Mom.
*Step Mom who?*
Step Mom, then slide to the right. See,
you're dancing!

· · ·

Knock, knock.
*Who's there?*
Cousin.
*Cousin who?*
Cousin and swearing is forbidden.

· · ·

Knock, knock.
*Who's there?*
Kin.
*Kin who?*
Kin anybody stop these knock-knock jokes?

Knock, knock.
*Who's there?*
Tissue.
*Tissue who?*
Sis asked, "Do you tare if I tissue?"

. . .

Knock, knock.
*Who's there?*
Sue.
*Sue who?*
Don't ask me, bro, I'm not a lawyer.

. . .

Knock, knock.
*Who's there?*
A-1.
*A–1 who?*
A-1 to know where Dad is.

. . .

Knock, knock.
*Who's there?*
Amusing.
*Amusing who?*
Hey Bro, amusing the phone right now!

Knock, knock.
*Who's there?*
Knoxville.
*Knoxville who?*
Uncle Knoxville always come to the door.

• • •

Knock, knock.
*Who's there?*
Vericose.
*Vericose who?*
Vericose family—we stick together.

• • •

Knock, knock.
*Who's there?*
Papa.
*Papa who?*
Paparazzi taking our picture.

• • •

Knock, knock.
*Who's there?*
Army.
*Army who?*
Army friends invited?

Knock, knock.
*Who's there?*
Oldest son.
*Oldest son who?*
"Oldest son shines bright on my old
    Kentucky home."

• • •

Knock, knock.
*Who's there?*
Step father.
*Step father who?*
You step father because you wear
    size thirteens.

• • •

Knock, knock.
*Who's there?*
Mama.
*Mama who?*
Mama told me there'd be days like this.

• • •

Knock, knock.
*Who's there?*
Army.
*Army who?*
Army and my family invited?

Knock, knock.
*Who's there?*
Kissin'.
*Kissin' who?*
Ever wonder about your kissin' cousins?

. . .

Knock, knock.
*Who's there?*
Tuba.
*Tuba who?*
Bro, can I borrow your tuba toothpaste?

. . .

Knock, knock.
*Who's there?*
Family.
*Family who?*
The door's always open to family.

. . .

Knock, knock.
*Who's there?*
Unk.
*Unk who?*
Don't believe the bunk about unk!

Knock, knock.
*Who's there?*
Your son.
*Your son who?*
Your son is pretty bright.

. . .

Knock, knock.
*Who's there?*
My brother-in-law.
*My brother-in-law who?*
My brother-in-law is an outlaw.

. . .

Knock, knock.
*Who's there?*
Cousin.
*Cousin who?*
My cousin is so mean, I'm almost cousin
    and using bad language.

# THIS & THAT

Knock, knock.
*Who's there?*
Tail.
*Tail who?*
Tail all your friends a knock-knock joke.

• • •

Knock, knock.
*Who's there?*
Deep.
*Deep who?*
Deep ends on who you were expecting.

Knock, knock.
*Who's there?*
Queasy.
*Queasy who?*
Queasy as 1-2-3!

. . .

Knock, knock.
*Who's there?*
Dummy.
*Dummy who?*
Dummy a favor, will you? Thanks.

. . .

Knock, knock.
*Who's there?*
Beckon.
*Beckon who?*
Beckon goes well with eggs.

. . .

Knock, knock.
*Who's there?*
Carfare.
*Carfare who?*
Carfare a slice of watermelon?

Knock, knock.
*Who's there?*
Quiche.
*Quiche who?*
Dracula gives the quiche of death!

. . .

Knock, knock.
*Who's there?*
Derby.
*Derby who?*
Derby a empty milk bottle in the fridge.

. . .

Knock, knock.
*Who's there?*
Dishes.
*Dishes who?*
Dishes the stupidest knock-knock joke ever!

. . .

Knock, knock.
*Who's there?*
Weiner.
*Weiner who?*
Weiner and still champion!

Knock, knock.
*Who's there?*
Avenue.
*Avenue who?*
Avenue heard the good news?

• • •

Knock, knock.
*Who's there?*
Beach.
*Beach who?*
Beach one be kind to everyone.

• • •

Knock, knock.
*Who's there?*
Demure.
*Demure who?*
Demure I get, demure I want!

• • •

Knock, knock.
*Who's there?*
Manor.
*Manor who?*
Are you a manor a mouse?

Knock, knock.
*Who's there?*
Diploma.
*Diploma who?*
Diploma is here to fix the sink.

• • •

Knock, knock.
*Who's there?*
Macho.
*Macho who?*
Macho do about nothing.

• • •

Knock, knock.
*Who's there?*
One.
*One who?*
One-der why you keep asking that?

• • •

Knock, knock.
*Who's there?*
A vet.
*A vet who?*
A vet ya vant to come in.

Knock, knock.
*Who's there?*
Recent.
*Recent who?*
Recent you a bill the first of the month.

• • •

Knock, knock.
*Who's there?*
Barn.
*Barn who?*
Barn to be wild!

• • •

Knock, knock.
*Who's there?*
Market.
*Market who?*
Market paid in full.

• • •

Knock, knock.
*Who's there?*
Diesel.
*Diesel who?*
Diesel be your bag on the step I suppose?

Knock, knock.
*Who's there?*
Blue.
*Blue who?*
Glad you blue your nose.

• • •

Knock, knock.
*Who's there?*
UCI.
*UCI who?*
UCI had to knock—there's no bell!

• • •

Knock, knock.
*Who's there?*
Arfer.
*Arfer who?*
Arfer-got!

• • •

Knock, knock.
*Who's there?*
Ferris.
*Ferris who?*
Ferris fair, so play right!

Knock, knock.
*Who's there?*
Ammonia.
*Ammonia who?*
Ammonia a lost person finding my way.

· · ·

Knock, knock.
*Who's there?*
Won.
*Won who?*
Won for the twee; the wain is falling!

· · ·

Knock, knock.
*Who's there?*
Diploma.
*Diploma who?*
Call diploma, the tub's overflowing!

· · ·

Knock, knock.
*Who's there?*
Police.
*Police who?*
Police, stop telling these knock-knock jokes!

Knock, knock.
*Who's there?*
Opera.
*Opera who?*
Opera-tunity is knocking!

• • •

Knock, knock.
*Who's there?*
Wah.
*Wah who?*
Well, you don't have to get so excited about it!

• • •

Knock, knock.
*Who's there?*
Dishes.
*Dishes who?*
Dishes the FBI, open up!

• • •

Knock, knock.
*Who's there?*
Chew chew.
*Chew chew who?*
Chew chew train delivers bubble gum.

Knock, knock.
*Who's there?*
Jam.
*Jam who?*
Jam 'n' bread.

. . .

Knock, knock.
*Who's there?*
Broom mates.
*Broom mates who?*
Broom mates are two witches living together.

. . .

Knock, knock.
*Who's there?*
Diesel.
*Diesel who?*
Diesel make you laugh, I promise!

. . .

Knock, knock.
*Who's there?*
Diesel.
*Diesel who?*
Diesel teach me to go around knocking on
doors!

Knock, knock.
*Who's there?*
Vasar girl.
*Vasar girl who?*
Vasar girl like you doing in a joke like this?

• • •

Knock, knock.
*Who's there?*
Dishes.
*Dishes who?*
Dishes your friend Margaret, so open the
door.

• • •

Knock, knock.
*Who's there?*
Dishes.
*Dishes who?*
Dishes getting boring.

• • •

Knock, knock.
*Who's there?*
Dozen.
*Dozen who?*
Dozen anyone want to be my friend?

Knock, knock.
*Who's there?*
House.
*House who?*
House-oon do you want to hear another
knock-knock joke?

• • •

Knock, knock.
*Who's there?*
Dozen.
*Do en who?*
Dozen anyone ever answer this door?

• • •

Knock, knock.
*Who's there?*
Anthem.
*Anthem who?*
Oh, you anthem boy you!

• • •

Knock, knock.
*Who's there?*
Argue.
*Argue who?*
Argue going to let me in or not?

Knock, knock.
*Who's there?*
Mammoth.
*Mammoth who?*
Mammoth is stuck 'cause I've been eatin'
    peanut butter!

• • •

Knock, knock.
*Who's there?*
I used.
*I used who?*
I used to be able to reach the doorbell.

• • •

Knock, knock.
*Who's there?*
Cargo.
*Cargo what?*
Cargo "beep, beep."

• • •

Knock, knock.
*Who's there?*
Wire.
*Wire who?*
Wire you just standing there? Let me in!

Knock, knock.
*Who's there?*
Ice.
*Ice who?*
Ice the guy who builds the boats, and Ice
the guy who sails 'em, too!

• • •

Knock, knock.
*Who's there?*
Dishwasher.
*Dishwasher who?*
Dishwasher the way I spoke before I got
false teeth.

• • •

Knock, knock.
*Who's there?*
Butter.
*Butter who?*
Butter late than never!

• • •

Knock, knock.
*Who's there?*
Tuna.
*Tuna who?*
Tuna piano and it will sound better.

Knock, knock.
*Who's there?*
Dishes.
*Dishes who?*
Dishes the very worst knock-knock joke I've
heard.

. . .

Knock, knock.
*Who's there?*
Disk.
*Disk who?*
Disk is a recording. Leave your message
after the beep!

. . .

Knock, knock.
*Who's there?*
Jester.
*Jester who?*
Jester minute, till I find my key.

# FINAL KNOCKS

Knock, knock.
*Who's there?*
Dummy.
*Dummy who?*
Dummy a favor and go away!

. . .

Knock, knock.
*Who's there?*
Let us.
*Let us who?*
Let us in and you'll find out!

Knock, knock.
*Who's there?*
Anvil.
*Anvil who?*
Anvil you tell me your name, too?

. . .

Knock, knock.
*Who's there?*
I love.
*I love who?*
I don't know. You tell me!

. . .

Knock, knock.
*Who's there?*
Pasture.
*Pasture who?*
Pasture bedtime, isn't it?

. . .

Knock, knock.
*Who's there?*
Nuisance.
*Nuisance who?*
What's nuisance yesterday?

Knock, knock.
*Who's there?*
Soda lady.
*Soda lady who?*
Quit your yodeling and let me in!

• • •

Knock, knock.
*Who's there?*
Handsome.
*Handsome who?*
Handsome spaghetti through the keyhole
and I'll tell you.

• • •

Knock, knock.
*Who's there?*
Disguise.
*Disguise who?*
Disguise the limit!

• • •

Knock, knock.
*Who's there?*
Says.
*Says who?*
Says me, that's who!

Knock, knock.
*Who's there?*
Dismay.
*Dismay who?*
Dismay be a knock-knock joke, but I'm not
    laughing.

. . .

Knock, knock.
*Who's there?*
Tinkerbell.
*Tinkerbell who?*
Tinkerbell is out of order.

. . .

Knock, knock.
*Who's there?*
Cash.
*Cash who?*
Cash me if you can!

. . .

Knock, knock.
*Who's there?*
Bless.
*Bless who?*
Thanks, but I didn't sneeze.

Knock, knock.
*Who's there?*
Adair.
*Adair who?*
Adair once, but now I'm bald.

. . .

Knock, knock.
*Who's there?*
Acid.
*Acid who?*
Acid down and be quiet!

. . .

Knock, knock.
*Who's there?*
Button.
*Button who?*
Button in is not polite.

. . .

Knock, knock.
*Who's there?*
Amish.
*Amish who?*
That's funny, you don't look like a shoe.

Knock, knock.
*Who's there?*
Dishes.
*Dishes who?*
Dishes the end of the world. Farewell!

• • •

Knock, knock.
*Who's there?*
Annapolis.
*Annapolis who?*
Annapolis my favorite fruit.

• • •

Knock, knock.
*Who's there?*
Nice toe.
*Nice toe who?*
"Nice toe meet you," said the foot doctor.

• • •

Knock, knock.
*Who's there?*
Amish.
*Amish who?*
Amish you very much.

Knock, knock.
*Who's there?*
Your maid.
*Your maid who?*
Your maid your bed, now lie in it.

• • •

Knock, knock.
*Who's there?*
Jewel.
*Jewel who?*
Jewel know when you open the door.

• • •

Knock, knock.
*Who's there?*
CD.
*CD who?*
CD badge? This is the police. Open up!

• • •

Knock, knock.
*Who's there?*
Hour.
*Hour who?*
Hour you today? I'm fine.

Knock, knock.
*Who's there?*
Oil.
*Oil who?*
Oil change my socks if I have to.

• • •

Knock, knock.
*Who's there?*
Cologne.
*Cologne who?*
Cologne me names won't help!

• • •

Knock, knock.
*Who's there?*
Collier.
*Collier who?*
Collier big brother and see if I care.

• • •

Knock, knock.
*Who's there?*
Canoe.
*Canoe who?*
Canoe come out and play?

Knock, knock.
*Who's there?*
Eureka.
*Eureka who?*
Eureka something bad, and it really stinks!

• • •

Knock, knock.
*Who's there?*
Cozy.
*Cozy who?*
Cozy who's knocking your door down.

• • •

Knock, knock.
*Who's there?*
Avenue.
*Avenue who?*
Avenue been missing me?

• • •

Knock, knock.
*Who's there?*
Toodle.
*Toodle who?*
Toodle-oo to you, too.

Knock, knock.
*Who's there?*
Datsun.
*Datsun who?*
Datsun old knock-knock joke.

• • •

Knock, knock.
*Who's there?*
Deluxe.
*Deluxe who?*
Deluxe Ness Monster.

• • •

Knock, knock.
*Who's there?*
Oscar and Greta.
*Oscar and Greta who?*
Oscar foolish question, and Greta foolish
    answer.

• • •

Knock, knock.
*Who's there?*
Omega.
*Omega who?*
Omega up your mind!

Knock, knock.
*Who's there?*
Schick.
*Schick who?*
Schick as a dog.

. . .

Knock, knock.
*Who's there?*
John.
*John who?*
John hands and make a circle.

. . .

Knock, knock.
*Who's there?*
Smee.
*Smee who?*
Smee, your brother.

. . .

Knock, knock.
*Who's there?*
Mommy.
*Mommy who?*
Mommy-easels are better now, can you
come over?

Knock, knock.
*Who's there?*
X.
*X who?*
X me no questions, I'll tell you no lies.

• • •

Knock, knock.
*Who's there?*
Fangs.
*Fangs who?*
"Fangs for letting me in," says Dracula.

• • •

Knock, knock.
*Who's there?*
Plow.
*Plow who?*
"Plow are you?" asked the farmer.

• • •

Knock, knock.
*Who's there?*
Spell.
*Spell who?*
W-H-O!

Knock, knock.
*Who's there?*
Two-Two.
*Two-Two who?*
Two-Two is a ballerina's dress.

. . .

Knock, knock.
*Who's there?*
Hippie.
*Hippie who?*
I'll have a hippie meal, please.

. . .

Knock, knock.
*Who's there?*
Juice.
*Juice who?*
Juice answer the door.

. . .

Knock, knock.
*Who's there?*
Lindy.
*Lindy who?*
Lindy me a cup of sugar, please.

Knock, knock.
*Who's there?*
Icy.
*Icy who?*
Icy London, icy France, icy someone's
　　underpants!

· · ·

　　　　　　Knock, knock.
　　　　　　*Who's there?*
　　　　　　Hype.
　　　　　　*Hype who?*
"Hype your runny nose," says the doctor.

· · ·

Knock, knock.
*Who's there?*
Scold.
*Scold who?*
It's scold at the North Pole.

· · ·

　　　　　　Knock, knock.
　　　　　　*Who's there?*
　　　　　　Rufus.
　　　　　　*Rufus who?*
Rufus leaking, get some buckets!

Knock, knock.
*Who's there?*
Sawyer.
*Sawyer who?*
The magician will sawyer in half!

• • •

Knock, knock.
*Who's there?*
Misty.
*Misty who?*
Misty bus, I'll have to walk.

• • •

Knock, knock.
*Who's there?*
Cheese.
*Cheese who?*
Cheese the girl of his dreams.

• • •

Knock, knock.
*Who's there?*
Diction.
*Diction who?*
Diction-ary helps you pronounce better.

Knock, knock.
*Who's there?*
Winnie.
*Winnie who?*
Winnie the poodle—I'm not a bear!

. . .

Knock, knock.
*Who's there?*
Mode.
*Mode who?*
Mode your lawn, now please pay me.

. . .

Knock, knock.
*Who's there?*
Justice.
*Justice who?*
Justice I suspected.

. . .

Knock, knock.
*Who's there?*
Fur.
*Fur who?*
Fur the last time—open the door!

# LIKE BIBLE TRIVIA?

Then check out these great books from
Barbour Publishing!


*My Final Answer* by Paul Kent
Thirty separate quizzes feature twelve multiple-choice
questions each—and the questions get progressively
harder!

> ISBN 1-58660-030-3/Paperback/256 pages/$2.97


*Bible IQ* by Rayburn Ray
One hundred sections of ten questions each—and a sys-
tematic scoring system to tell you just how well you did.

> ISBN 1-57748-837-7/Paperback/256 pages/$2.97


*Test Your Bible Knowledge* by Carl Shoup
Over 1,400 multiple-choice questions to test your met-
tle, tickle your funny bone, and tantalize your intellect.

> ISBN 1-55748-541-0/Paperback/224 pages/$2.97


*Fun Facts about the Bible* by Robyn Martins
Challenging and intriguing Bible trivia—expect some
of the answers to surprise you!

> ISBN 1-55748-897-5/Paperback/256 pages/$2.97

———————————

Available wherever books are sold.
Or order from:

Barbour Publishing, Inc.
P.O. Box 719
Uhrichsville, OH 44683

If you order by mail, add $2.00 to your order for shipping.
Prices subject to change without notice.